Relentless SPIRITUALITY

EMBRACING THE SPIRITUAL DISCIPLINES OF A.B. SIMPSON

GARY KEISLING

D1157591

CHRISTIAN PUBLICATIONS, INC.
CAMP HILL, PENNSYLVANIA

✠ CHRISTIAN PUBLICATIONS, INC.

3825 Hartzdale Drive, Camp Hill, PA 17011
www.christianpublications.com

Faithful, biblical publishing since 1883

Relentless Spirituality
ISBN: 0-87509-974-2
LOC Control Number: 2004102516
© 2004 by Gary Keisling
All rights reserved
Printed in the United States of America

04   05   06   07   08   5   4   3   2   1

DEDICATION

To the men and women who invested in my spiritual formation and development out of their love and faithfulness to Jesus Christ.

To those sharing the journey with me, challenging and inspiring me to continue reaching higher, going further and growing deeper in my relationship with the Lord.

To the people who will be the instruments in God's hands to bring about the new things God has in store for me.

To my wife, Sue, my faithful companion and friend in the life and on the journey we share together as servants of Jesus Christ.

To my children, Robert and Beth, with the hope and prayer that the life and example your mother and I have set before you continues to direct your path in the steps and the ways of Jesus Christ.

CONTENTS

The writer of the New Testament book of Hebrews exhorts us not to be "sluggish, but imitators of those who through faith and patience inherit the promises" (6:12, NASB). He tells us to "remember those who led you, who spoke the word of God to you; and considering the result of their conduct, imitate their faith" (13:7, NASB).

Obviously, then, to know and to imitate those who have stood before us and with us in the power and character of Jesus Christ is a major part of what we can do to succeed in walking *our* path with Christ in our times. For myself, at least, awareness and understanding of the lives of Christ's great people, who have walked with Him through the ages, has been indispensable for opening and steadying my vision of what is possible for the disciple of Jesus. These treasures of Christ, living and dead, often surrounded by "the inhuman dearth of noble natures," as the poet Keats called it, have made me know that more—much more—is possible for us, and that this "much more" is what God has really intended for us.

Gary Keisling has now made accessible once again the person and life of A.B. Simpson. Simpson was a person of incredible talents and towering intellect who learned in the life of a pastor and world Christian leader how to be with Jesus and fully be His man. This book is correctly titled *Relentless Spirituality*, for that is what characterized Simpson. And his spirituality was not ethereal and merely of words, thoughts and feelings. He truly "embraced the spiritual disciplines" in the most substantial and concrete of ways. He understood that the central focus of Christian spirituality was obedience to Christ in every facet of life. And he understood that such obedience came through specific practices which opened the sluice gates of grace upon the individual.

As you read this book you must first just sit back and enjoy the beauty of Simpson's life in Christ. Let it seize you. Let it draw you in. Know that you will learn from Simpson how to live life in the kingdom of heaven *now*. Such a life is the greatest opportunity for human beings on earth.

But then, as our passages from Hebrews say: Imitate Simpson. Do the things he did. The failure to do this is the number-one reason why we do not carry through to the quality of life of the great ones in Christ. *We simply do not do what they did.*

I have known numerous people who made the trip to India to talk, or even work for a while, with the late Mother Theresa of Calcutta. But it seems never to occur to them that they should find out how she became the Christ-bearer she was, and that they then should do what she did to live the life in Christ she did.

That is the key. The subtitle of this book is: "Embracing the Spiritual Disciplines of A.B. Simpson." The author has given us a rich portion of Simpson's life and words. Now we can imitate him as he imitated Christ (see 1 Corinthians 11:1, NASB). And, "be imitators of God, as beloved children" (Ephesians 5:1, NASB).

We might begin, as Simpson did, in *submission* and in *sacrifice*. Submission meant to will only what Christ willed. We can practice living that way. It would not be deprivation, but fulfillment. In Simpson's words, which begin the first chapter of this book, "Live for the life to come. Live in the light of eternity. Live for the powers of the age to come."[1] This means to live now in the reality of God's kingdom. It is always a matter of releasing the lesser to seize upon the greater. And in the light of this, sacrifice, though often painful—or even, for the moment, paralyzing—is the sure doorway to "the life that is life indeed."

Simpson knew that God was active and ever-present in his life and ministry. His understanding of the reality of the Spirit of God in action led naturally to his involvement in healing prayer as well as world evangelization and the teaching of the importance of "alliance" among God's scattered people. In this respect, his work and message has never been more relevant than it is today.

The importance of the physical body to spirituality, as well as the role of imagination and creativity, fit right into Simpson's holistic understanding of life in Christ. He understood that personal victory over sin and failure was more important than his work as a minister. He was integrity through and through, which stood him in good stead in the very difficult battles he often faced. Christ stood with him and he in Christ. He was perpetually "restless" for Christ "Himself."

May this lovely book reawaken us to what life in Christ can be and to how the disciplines of the spiritual life enable us to "grow in the grace and knowledge of our Lord and Savior Jesus Christ" (2 Peter 3:18, NASB).

—Dallas Willard

INTRODUCTION

We often view the "defining moment" of a person's life through the prism of a single unforgettable snapshot that forever captures our hearts and minds. The words "Let's roll!" immediately bring to mind the heroic actions of Todd Beamer and the other courageous passengers aboard the September 11 Flight 93 who averted a catastrophic disaster from occurring in our nation's capital.

Although we remember Todd Beamer and people like him by the defining moment of their lives, we recognize that their actions in that moment are the sum total of their characters. Their responses to the circumstances, events and opportunities life had dealt them molded and shaped the characters of the people we remember by that defining moment.

Have you ever wondered about what prepares a person for the defining moment that touches the lives of other people and may alter the course of history?

I have. I especially wonder about it when it comes to the men and women who touch the lives of countless numbers of people with the transforming power of God's love. The significance of their influence is not measured by the length of a story on the evening news or the placement of an article in the newspaper. Their influence is seen in lives that are transformed by the Lord's compassion and grace.

My curiosity has nothing to do with merely wanting to know what takes place to prepare a person for the moment when it comes his way. I have wondered because there is value in embracing the formative influences God uses to shape and mold the lives of men and women who follow in Christ's steps. I have wondered because God is concerned about forming the life of Christ in me, just as God is concerned about forming Christ's life in you.

Richard Foster's *Celebration of Discipline* and Dallas Willard's *The Spirit of the Disciplines* challenged the Christian community to rediscover the formative forces God uses to shape the character of Christ in our lives. They summon us to look beyond the defining moments or the "crisis events" to the underlying process of spiritual formation already taking place through the practice and the pursuit of the spiritual disciplines.

Sometimes the sheer significance of defining moments and crisis events obscures the recollection of the elements God's Spirit uses in bringing spiritual formation to pass. We overlook the underlying spiritual elements and dynamics the Lord is using in the process.

This seems to be the case with the life of a leading missionary statesman of the nineteenth century. The life and ministry of A.B. Simpson are frequently remembered by recalling the defining moments that characterized the ongoing developments in his relationship with and service to Jesus Christ. Simpson understood the danger of becoming fascinated or preoccupied with monumental experiences. He realized that the life of Christ is formed within us day-by-day. He expressed his concern for the daily process of spiritual formation through the habits and patterns of daily spiritual life by saying, "There is the continual receiving, breath by breath and moment by moment, between those long intervals and more marked experiences. This daily supply is even more needful to spiritual steadfastness and health."[1]

Simpson's words underscore the crucial importance of placing the focus on the daily patterns of one's spiritual life. The practices, habits and disciplines of life that facilitate the inflow of Christ's life into a person's being are the vital elements of his daily supply.

The significance of the defining moments in Simpson's life, or that of any spiritual leader, is best understood by considering the spiritual dynamics beneath the surface. The movement of God's Spirit upon the human heart unfolds within the flow of the individual's personal spiritual journey. The seed is sown before a harvest is reaped. Favorable conditions make germination possible. In God's time growth occurs and fruit is borne. Defining moments are the culmination of the Spirit's invisible working within the heart, mind, soul and spirit of the one who walks with God. Through His work, the individual's personal habits enter into a deeper relationship with Him, and as He lovingly imposes discipline, spiritual character is shaped and molded.

Come; join me for a look behind the defining moments into the life and patterns of spiritual formation that characterized one of the leading missionary statesmen of modern times. Let's discover the process of A.B. Simpson's spiritual formation by considering some of the spiritual disciplines that characterized the life and ministry of this innovative missionary pioneer. In doing so, may we learn to draw closer into the presence of the Lord.

First, we will consider Simpson's understanding of the Spirit's discipline in a believer's life and the role the disciplines play in spiritual formation. Second, we will highlight the role the disciplines of engagement played in cultivating Simpson's spiritual character. Finally, we will look at Simpson's personal practice and teaching concerning the pursuit of activities of the mind and body to benefit the spirit. These are known as disciplines of abstinence.

The Spirit, Discipline and Spiritual Disciplines

TEACH ME, LORD!

The Spirit and the *Disciplines* of Living

"*L* ive for the life to come. Live in the light of eternity. Live for the powers of the age to come."[1]

These words are not a pious, sermonic exhortation to God's people concerning the things they ought to do. Rather, they declare A.B. Simpson's challenge to the Church to follow his lead in focusing life's course upon the pursuit of the eternal. Accepting this challenge calls for the courage to make a bold, definitive decision. It is a decision to embrace spiritual disciplines and to make all things subordinate to the value of knowing God intimately and continuously growing in Christ's grace.

The Apostle Paul's rousing words, "train yourself to be godly" (1 Timothy 4:7), challenged Timothy to make this formative decision. Simply responding to life's circumstances and events is an inadequate and unacceptable strategy for spiritual development. Scripture implores us to be wise and faithful stewards of the grace we have received. As faithful stewards we have a responsibility to establish an intentional course leading to our own personal spiritual development and the spiritual growth of Christ's body, the Church (see Ephesians 4:12-13).

Paul's admonition to Timothy flowed out of the conscious decision he had already made to "consider everything a loss compared to the surpassing greatness of knowing Christ Jesus" (Philippians 3:8). Nothing was more important to Paul than knowing Jesus Christ. Paul had established the ultimate priority in his life. This settled priority authenticated the validity of his exhortations to pursue the things leading to godliness. The words "follow my example, as I follow the example of Christ" (1 Corinthians 11:1) are an open invitation to join Paul in pursuing the formation of Christ's character and life within our own lives.

This was an invitation Albert Benjamin Simpson could not refuse. He wholeheartedly accepted Paul's invitation. Simpson made a conscious and deliberate decision to forsake anything that had the potential to jeopardize the pursuit of his spiritual formation, service to Christ and a life leading to godliness. Throughout his life, in the midst of various and often difficult circumstances, Simpson made decisions which continuously reaffirmed his commitment to follow in Paul's steps. It is out of a life of obedient submission to Christ that A.B. Simpson invited others to "live in the light of eternity." His invitation expressed the longing of his heart for every believer to enter into the joyous satisfaction of the fullness of Christ.

To this end, Simpson understood and embraced the role of discipline in his own life. He extolled the importance of voluntarily embracing practices and habits that enhance spiritual development and lead to godliness. Simpson did so without any fear of reverting to some form of legalism. He knew the disciplines were a gift of God's grace that he voluntarily embraced in cooperation with the Spirit's working to form Christ's character within his own being.

A.B. Simpson's writings are seasoned with statements underscoring the value he placed on practicing the spiritual disciplines. Their flavoring is a reflection of the practices he embraced in his life with Christ. These statements give us a glimpse into Simpson's heart. We discover that he was a man who was not afraid to bare his soul, letting us see the longing desire of his heart in a way that dispels any notions of spiritual superiority. He openly said, "I had to learn to take my spiritual life from Jesus every moment."[2] These are the words of a man growing in godliness. They reveal an openness, an enticing vulnerability inviting, even compelling, us to join him in pursuing activities of spiritual formation leading us into the likeness of Jesus Christ.

DAILY SUPPLY

Moment-by-moment, day-by-day we must learn what it means to take our life from Jesus. Simpson called this his "daily supply." His unpublished poem "Breathing Out and Breathing In" describes his attempt to cultivate a conscious awareness of Christ's presence living within.

> Jesus, breathe Thy Spirit on me,
> Teach me how to breathe Thee in,
> Help me pour into Thy bosom
> All my life of self and sin.
>
> I am breathing out my own life,
> That I may be filled with Thine;
> Letting go my strength and weakness,
> Breathing in Thy life divine.
>
> Breathing out my sinful nature,
> Thou has borne it all for me;
> Breathing in Thy cleansing fullness
> Finding all my life in Thee.
>
> I am breathing out my sorrow
> On Thy kind and gentle breast;
> Breathing in Thy joy and comfort,
> Breathing in Thy peace and rest.
>
> I am breathing out my sickness,
> Thou hast borne its burden too;
> I am breathing in Thy healing,
> Ever promised, ever new.
>
> I am breathing out my longings
> In Thy listening, loving ear;
> I am breathing in Thy answers,
> Stilling every doubt and fear.
>
> I am breathing every moment,
> Drawing all my life from Thee;
> Breath by breath I live upon Thee,
> Blessed Spirit, breathe in me.
>
> I am breathing out my sorrow,
> Breathing out my sin;
> I am breathing, breathing, breathing
> All Thy fullness in.[3]

Simpson never considered the conscious awareness of Christ's presence and reliance upon Him for the "daily supply" as an end in itself. Without dismissing the significance of this "daily supply" in the believer's consecration and edification, it is more than this. It is the essential source and qualifying criterion for empowering God's children for service and ministry in advancing Christ's kingdom. Simpson understood the crucial correlation between spiritual character and effectiveness in ministry. This relationship is too important to ignore or dismiss as inconsequential. Simpson realized that evangelistic effectiveness was proportional to the quality of the spiritual life and experience of those who preached, labored and prayed for the salvation of men and women to become members of God's kingdom.[4]

His vision and determination to reach the lost could not be compromised by spiritual indifference or lethargy within the Church. He denounced what he perceived to be a low level of spirituality in the Church by saying, "The blight of the Church today is spiritual starvation. People are famishing on rationalism, socialism, sensationalism, on lifeless bonds and bank notes and unwholesome pleasures."[5] Simpson did not make statements such as this in a derogatory or condemnatory manner. They were made within the context of an appeal to pursue the things leading to godliness and the advancement of Christ's kingdom.

To A.B. Simpson, the fulfillment of the Great Commission and the sanctification of God's children were inseparable. The vitality of one's spiritual life, the journey and progress in spiritual formation, have profound ramifications for the individual, the congregation and the harvest waiting to be reaped. He would most certainly concur with R. Kent Hughes' assertion that

> Whether or not we have disciplined ourselves will make a huge difference in this life. We are all members of one another, and we are each elevated or depressed by the inner lives of one another. Some of us affect others like a joyous tide, lifting them upward, but some of us are like an undertow to the Body of Christ.[6]

It is the upward redeeming influence Simpson sought to exert for Christ. This is affirmed by the role of sanctification within his own life and as a distinctive doctrinal characteristic of The Christian and Missionary Alliance. Simpson's pursuit of godliness in his own life compelled him to take the gospel of Christ to the unreached people of the world.

DEVELOPING SPIRITUALLY

Evangelization and sanctification are not objectives Simpson sought to accomplish on his own. They were activities he pursued in obedient dependence upon Christ and in cooperation with the Holy Spirit. He understood the Father's concern for the lost and the spiritual development of His children.

A.B. Simpson recognized that the Father's love for His children compelled the Spirit to actively seek ways to further the believer's spiritual formation through the circumstances and events of life. Commenting on Jacob's spiritual formation, Simpson notes:

> When Jacob yielded himself up to the Presence in the submission of perfect trust, then came the fullness of God's working and God's victorious love. We too must learn that the secret of our deepest desires after God is His overruling grace.[7]

Simpson sees God playing an active role within the believer's life, cultivating the desire for continued spiritual development that ultimately culminates in the maturity and character of the fullness of Christ. It also culminates in action, seeking to reach others with the Father's love and grace through Jesus Christ.

Since Jacob's severest trials came after his consecration at Peniel (see Genesis 32:22-32), Simpson fully expected the same to be true for others. It was true in his own spiritual development. After he completely yielded himself to Christ, Simpson perceived spiritual realities in a new light. The surrendered heart has the spiritual sensitivity to perceive and recognize the Father's interactive involvement in life's circumstances and events that are designed to further our development in Christlikeness. Consequently, it may seem as though God has a greater level of interactive involvement in our spiritual formation following our own personal surrender and consecration to Christ.

Simpson expresses this personal realization of God's longing desire for his own spiritual formation by writing:

> The Holy Spirit is not leading us to develop our goodness, strength
> and love, but to discover our insufficiency and make room for a
> new manifestation of Christ's sufficiency and grace. In this holy
> discipline the Spirit uses all the circumstances of our life as the
> framework in which to constantly manifest and exhibit the face of
> Jesus Christ and the fullness of His grace. Trials and temptations
> only furnish new channels, needs and opportunities for the Mas-
> ter to live out His life within us. As the potter turns the wheel and
> at the same time molds the clay, so God's providences are the
> whole of life and the Holy Spirit the molding hand of the potter.[8]

The lesson embedded upon Jeremiah's heart and mind while
he stood watching the potter work the clay, listening to God's
voice (see Jeremiah 18), was ablaze within Simpson's soul. An
attitude and posture of trusting submission to God's sovereign
working, even in the face of mysteries he did not yet understand,
governed his understanding of God's interactive involvement in
his own spiritual formation. It prompted him to write these
words of counsel:

> The first thing you need in order to be of any use anywhere is to
> be thoroughly broken, completely subjected and utterly crucified
> in the very core and center of your will. Then you will accept dis-
> cipline and learn to yield and obey so that He can use you as a
> flexible and perfectly adjusted instrument. Henceforth you will
> only do what God wills and choose only what God chooses.[9]

These words underscore the premium Simpson placed on the
surrendered life, a life lived in complete submission to the will of
the Father. Some of life's most valuable lessons are learned in the
hard places and through experiences we would not choose. Consequently, Simpson invites us to join him in living in trustful, obedient submission to God. He cautions against the possibility of
missing "the discipline of life and the victories of faith if we do not
watch for God in all the hard places that come to us day by day."[10]
He writes,

> Look at the hard places in our lives not as discouragements, but
> as challenges, things that God has permitted that He may over-
> come them. And that we may be lifted through the conflict to a
> higher place of victorious strength and blessing.[11]

A.B. Simpson recognized that God had more in mind than his own spiritual formation. While recognizing the importance of his development in Christ, Simpson looked beyond himself to see the purpose God sought to accomplish through him. That purpose was the spiritual development of others. He writes,

> After God has pressed into a life by the long and hard process of trial and discipline, the influences of His grace and the power of His transforming Spirit, then He loves to take out of that life the same power and expend it on others. Power can never be lost; so if we receive of God's fullness we can no more help giving it out than the sun stop shining.[12]

Simpson never viewed the spiritual formation and growth God sought to bring into his life with an attitude of self-indulgence or spiritual favor. He repudiated the notion of sacrifice, even self-sacrifice, where it was needless, and declared it wrong.[13] Consequently, it is reasonable to assert that Simpson would have drawn the same conclusion concerning any spiritual discipline that was practiced in a similar fashion.

Simpson understood the Father's involvement in shaping his spiritual character as a sacred trust, equipping and rendering him effective in service to Christ and the advancement of His kingdom within the Church and throughout the world. He affirmed that there may be occasions when God lovingly imposes restraints upon us in order to bring us into conformity with the good the Creator has for us. Simpson viewed the restraints God imposes as a loving limitation that directs us into spiritually beneficial avenues.

Leading people into a personal relationship with Jesus Christ and into the depths of the Christ-life are two primary objectives Simpson connected with spiritual discipline. This is why he could view difficult circumstances in light of the opportunities for spiritual formation that came through those experiences. "How can we become more than conquerors? We can get out of the conflict a spiritual discipline that will greatly strengthen our faith and establish our spiritual character."[14]

This exhortation reveals Simpson's commitment to practice personally the spiritual disciplines. It affirms his conscious and deliberate decision to pursue the things leading to godliness simultaneously and in cooperation with the Spirit's working to mold and shape his spiritual character. Expressing this in the first-person plural pronoun "we" reveals his concern for the spiritual formation of other believers.

The realization that he had a sacred responsibility to bring others into the fullness of the Christ-life never escaped Simpson's attention. His concern for the spiritual formation of others permeates his writings. Simpson's works are authentic spiritual theology. They do not present abstract theology, but expound biblical truth with a view to the spiritual formation of the readers.[15] His sermons, books, poetry and hymns are concerned with the spiritual transformation of people. Simpson's spiritual purpose was to guide people into the fullness of the Christ-life, and then into the full expression of Christ's life in the world.[16]

In *The Christ Life* Simpson outlined practical steps Christians can take in furthering their own spiritual formation. He developed them in a way that underscores the conscious, deliberate and active role believers play in furthering their own spiritual development. These steps are an autobiographical testimony to an aspect of the process A.B. Simpson pursued in his own spiritual formation.

> [Life in Him] must be a momentary life, not a current that flows on through its own momentum; but a succession of little acts and habits . . . so that if you shall renew this fellowship every moment, you shall always abide in Him. . . . [T]his abiding must be established by a succession of definite acts of will, and of real, fixed, steadfast trust in Christ. It does not come as a spontaneous and irresistible impulse that carries you whether you will or not, but you have to begin by an act of trust, and must repeat it until it becomes a habit.[17]

These words of personal testimony affirm the necessity of conscious little *acts* in establishing the foundation to cultivate a *habit*. Over time the movement from an *act* to a *habit* repeated with sufficient frequency becomes an established pattern in one's spiritual formation. Eventually, the established pattern becomes as unconscious as breathing itself. Over time it becomes a distinctive trait, a part of one's character, a vital and indispensable element in one's life and relationship with Jesus Christ.

In *Echoes of the New Creation*, Simpson writes:

> In practicing the presence of God slowly and patiently, the habit of dependence is formed; it is there that we triumph or fall. Cultivate the habit of constant dependence. In everything let it be, "Not I, but Christ," until at last it becomes so natural that you do it without thinking, that almost mechanically you will find yourself saying, "Jesus for this," "What shall I do, Lord?" Thus we shall establish the habit of dependency upon Him for all the little details.[18]

Simpson's words underscore his conviction that Christians play an active role in their own spiritual development. There is nothing passive about it. Christ's followers must seize every opportunity to grow in the grace of God. In *A Larger Christian Life*, he describes our participation by saying:

> While it is true that all the resources are divinely provided, this does not justify a spirit of passive negligence on our part. In fact, it summons us all the more to diligence and earnestness in pressing forward in our spiritual career. . . .
>
> [Salvation] is an inward principle of life that must be developed in every part of our life, and to this we are to "make every effort" (2 Peter 1:5), an effort that often reaches the extent of "fear and trembling." When this happens, there rises a holy and solemn sense of responsibility to make the most of our spiritual resources and opportunities, because "it is God who works in [us]."[19]

Making the most of the resources and opportunities given to us is a critical determining factor in spiritual development. Individual responsiveness and responsibility play vital roles in the believer's own spiritual formation. Simpson notes:

> Every servant is given, at the beginning of his spiritual life, an equal measure of spiritual resource, and that the difference in the issues of human lives is not to be found in the unequal measure of grace and power afforded from on high, but in the unequal measure in which they have improved the power given.[20]

His comments reveal personal responsibility, steps and a structure to follow that are consistent with the pursuit and practice of spiritual disciplines. He maintains that what we become through the provisions and grace of Jesus Christ depends upon us. For Simpson, the practice of God's presence through inward prayer and bringing His presence into every thought and activity of life and service is at the heart of the Christ-life.[21]

In taking these steps Simpson did not depart from his fundamental convictions concerning the grace of God.

> [Sanctification] is not the work of man nor means, nor of our own strugglings, but His prerogative. It is the gift of the Holy Ghost, the fruit of the Spirit, the grace of the Lord Jesus Christ, the prepared inheritance of all who will enter in, the great obtainment of faith, not the attainment of works. . . . It is the inflow into man's being of the life and purity of the infinite, eternal Holy One, bringing His own perfection and working out in us His own will.[22]

Spiritual formation is not something we accomplish on our own. It is actualized by the enabling power of the Holy Spirit. The Spirit is the actualizer in practicing the presence of God.[23]

Simpson's position has much in common with Richard Foster's statement that views the disciplines as tools in our spiritual formation, and our spiritual life itself as gifts of God: "God has given us the Disciplines of the spiritual life as a means of receiving His grace. The Disciplines allow us to place ourselves before God so He can transform us."[24] The transformation of our character and being into the likeness, stature, fullness and maturity of Christ is the Lord's doing.

It is in this spirit that Simpson advocated the principle of *separation*. He viewed separation as an inherent and indispensable dimension of consecration and sanctification. One must separate and abstain from the things of this world so there can be a complete and total dedication to God. Separating or abstaining even from activities to further the work of God's grace in our lives is paramount to Simpson's beliefs, teaching and practice. The principle of abstinence played a significant role in his continued spiritual formation.

He called upon believers to do more than renounce and separate themselves from evil in all of its many and varied forms. He called upon believers to separate themselves from things that are not sinful in and of themselves, but which could be things that impede one's spiritual development in the Christ-life.

> The aim and motive must be separated from all that is not for His glory; the source of its pleasure must be purified and the spirit separated from all joy that is not in harmony with the joy of the Lord.
>
> Is your spirit thus separated, cleansed and detached from everything that could defile or distract you from the will of God and life of holiness?[25]

This separation Simpson was calling for is abstinence. He challenged us to abstain voluntarily from the things of life so we may pursue a higher purpose.

This higher purpose is dedicating ourselves to the fulfillment of God's design for our lives and within our lives. It is not enough merely to practice abstinence or separation. The next step must be taken. This step involves a conscious and deliberate dedication of ourselves to God. "Therefore, I urge you, brothers, in view of God's mercy, to offer your bodies as living sacrifices, holy and pleasing to God—this is your spiritual act of worship" (Romans 12:1).

Dedicating ourselves to God was central to Simpson's understanding of consecration and sanctification.

> We offer ourselves to God for His absolute ownership, that He may possess us as His peculiar property, prepare us for His purpose and work out in us all His holy and perfect will. . . . This is what the term consecration properly means. It is the voluntary surrender or self-offering of the heart, by the constraint of love to be the Lord's.[26]

By using plural pronouns "we" and "us," Simpson confirmed that he was not merely telling us what to do. The plural pronouns affirm that Simpson considered this a journey we are taking together. He was inviting us to join him on an adventure into the depths of the Christ-life. The invitation flowed from his conviction that God wants "us to give Him the possibilities of our lives and to let Him build upon them His own structure. He will construct temples of holiness that He will make His abode."[27]

A.B. Simpson never viewed this as an instantaneous accomplishment. A number of factors may impede the progress. God's desire for our lives may be met with reluctance. Even when we are open and responsive to the Spirit's leading, there are times when it is necessary to pause and reflect upon the things the Lord is teaching us. We may have to grasp the principles, comprehend the implications, understand the significance and live to the level of truth that has been entrusted to us before the Spirit can lead us deeper and further into the things of Christ. Simpson notes:

> It is here that the gradual phase of sanctification comes in. Commencing with a complete separation from evil and a complete dedication to God, sanctification now advances into all the fullness of Christ. It grows up to the measure of the stature of perfect personhood in Him, until every part of our beings is filled with God and becomes a channel to receive, a medium to reflect His grace and glory.[28]

More than anything else Simpson wanted his life and ministry to reflect the glory of Jesus Christ. To this end, he engaged in a variety of spiritual disciplines. Seeking to cooperate with the Spirit's sovereign working, Simpson availed himself of the disciplines as tools to aid in his spiritual formation. He knew that the Lord was working to shape and mold him. He wanted to cooperate with the Spirit's working no matter what the cost. His early hymns expressed the urgency of his desire to deepen his life in Christ, to grow in the Lord and to make himself available to God's service. These hymns required action and deeper commitment to the Lord.[29] "Search Me, O God" reveals his longing for more of Christ:

> Search me, O God, search me and know my heart,
> Try me and prove me in the hidden part;
> Cleanse me and make me holy, as Thou art,
> And lead me in the way everlasting.
>
> Thou art the same today and yesterday,
> Oh, make Thy life in me the same alway,
> Take from my heart the things that pass away;
> Lead, lead me in the way everlasting.
>
> Take my poor heart and only let me love
> The things that always shall abiding prove;

Bind all my heartstrings to the world above,
And lead me in the way everlasting.

Help me to lay my treasures upon high;
Teach me to seek my future in the sky;
Give me my portion yonder by and by,
And lead me in the way everlasting.

Oh, let my work abide the testing day
That shall consume the stubble and the hay;
Oh, build my house upon the rock, I pray,
And lead me in the way everlasting.[30]

Simpson wanted nothing less than to be and to live in the center of God's will, bringing honor and glory to Christ through every facet and dimension of his life and ministry. It is for this purpose that he embraced the discipline of the Spirit. And it is in this spirit that he invited us to join him in cooperating with the Spirit and in practicing the disciplines so Christ's character can be developed within us and His mission accomplished through us. Simpson's invitation comes through the example his life sets before us. It is proclaimed in his writings, and the invitation is voiced in hymns of aspiration that extol the virtues of a life totally surrendered to the Lord Jesus Christ.

A.B. Simpson called us to live for the honor, glory and praise of Jesus Christ. To follow in his steps means that we must embrace the discipline of the Spirit and pursue the practice of the spiritual disciplines leading to and resulting in the formation of the Christ-life within us. Let us consider the role spiritual disciplines played in Simpson's spiritual development, not out of curiosity or merely for the sake of knowing, but with a view toward our own spiritual formation and the glory of Christ our Lord.

CONSIDERATIONS FOR YOUR SPIRITUAL DEVELOPMENT

God is interested in developing the life of Christ within you. Working together in harmonious cooperation, the Father, the Son and the Holy Spirit will proactively seek to influence your spiritual formation and development.

Christians are always in the process of becoming. We will continue "until we all reach unity in the faith and in the knowledge of the Son of God and become mature, attaining to the whole measure of the fullness of Christ" (Ephesians 4:13). Our spiritual formation unfolds as God works within us, through us and in a partnership with us.

God's wisdom and knowledge will play a crucial role in determining how this unfolds in our lives. The vital issues are how we respond and the initiative we put forth in developing our life with Christ.

Let's consider our role.

First, we have to trust God. Of course, sometimes it is easier to *say* we trust God than it is to actually trust Him. Trusting the Lord for our salvation is one thing, but trusting Him enough to relinquish control of our lives is something else! Sometimes we want to reserve the right to have the last word or to veto something that is not to our liking.

● ● ● ● ● ● ● ● ● ● ● *Application*

1. Do you ever sense the tendency to hold back or have another plan, just in case God doesn't come through the way you want? What does this say about trust?
2. Sometimes God chooses to use things in our spiritual formation that we wouldn't choose, things that may be unpleasant or bring pain into our lives. How do you respond when this happens? Do you embrace it, confident in God's love for you, or do you ask, "Why me, Lord? Why me?"
3. Can you recall times when you questioned what God was doing? If so, how did you resolve it?
4. The second part of our role is our initiative, the conscious, deliberate effort we make to grow in Christ. Have you developed a personal spiritual growth plan for the coming year? If so, will the plan stretch you, or is it overly aggressive? (Plans that are too ambitious can be self-defeating.)

5. Develop a list of the things you are doing that are designed to help you develop spiritually (e.g., Bible study, prayer, accountability group or partner). What priority do you give to pursuing these things?
6. What will you let go of, give up or abstain from doing in order to develop spiritually?

Disciplines
of Engagement

Chapter
TWO

LEARNING TO TRUST
The Place of *Submission* in Life with Christ

he model for the discipline of submission is Jesus Christ. Jesus' words, "Father . . . may your will be done" (Matthew 26:42), exemplify His submission to the Father's authority and will. His life models His expectation for those who would follow Him. "If anyone would come after me, he must deny himself and take up his cross daily and follow me" (Luke 9:23). The apostles' words echo His teaching, indicating that we are to have the same attitude as Jesus, who made Himself nothing, assumed the nature of a servant and was obedient unto death (see Philippians 2:1-11). Their writings summon us to follow their example as they follow Christ (see 1 Corinthians 11:1). Submission sets us free from the tyranny of needing to have our own way. It liberates us to live under the loving authority of the One who loves us and who died for us, so we might live to the glory of God.

Apart from the discipline of submission it is impossible to know the fullness of the Christ-life. Knowing Jesus Christ as Savior frees us from the bondage of sin and death (see Romans 8:2). We are no longer under Satan's authority; our lives are under the authority of the Spirit, who lives within us (see 8:9-11). We are free to give our lives back to God as living sacrifices (see 12:1) just as the Son gave His life to the Father.

Simpson pointed to the example of Christ in His appeal to Christians to embrace submission. In summoning us to submit, Simpson realized that embracing submission as a spiritual discipline opens the door for it to become a way of life.

> Jesus, who walked this earth as our Example, never tried to be
> independent, but He constantly received His Father's life, drew

His being from His Father, and lived by Him. . . . So He wants you and me to live in Him. He is just repeating the life He lived . . . utterly dependent, an empty vessel, receiving all from above. So, now, He requires you and me to be empty vessels, receiving all from Him.[1]

Jesus is seeking to reproduce His life in us. This requires more than merely acknowledging that this is Jesus' desire. It involves surrender to the will, purpose and plan of Christ the Lord. We must yield ourselves to the Master's leading.

Submitting to Christ's authority is the essential element that distinguishes the practice of the spiritual disciplines from the self-improvement schemes men devise. Apart from submission to Christ's authority, spiritual disciplines are little more than works of the flesh. They may have some transitory temporal benefit, but in and of themselves they do not have the power or the capability to transform one's eternal character or the destiny of the soul. Simpson noted,

> The Christian life is not self-improving, but it is wholly supernatural and Divine. Now the resurrection cannot come until there has been death. This is presupposed, and just as real as the death has been will be the measure of the resurrection life and power. Do not fear, therefore, to die and to die to all that should be left behind, and to die to self and really cease to be. We lose nothing by letting go, and we cannot enter in till we come out. If we be dead with Him, we shall also live with Him.[2]

Submission to Christ's authority is an issue every believer must settle. The place where submission to Christ's authority may begin to be resolved is within the home and family, the first "human authority" God established. The extent of a person's submission to Christ's authority may be seen in the attitude and response displayed in that setting. The submission learned there can play a vital role in a person's spiritual formation.

A.B. Simpson recalled an incident involving a personal desire that was contrary to his parents' will. They expressly forbade him to do something. His parents' stance may have seemed unreasonable, but it flowed out of their love for their son and the desire to protect and shield him from the tragic consequences that befell others. Pretending to concede to their wishes, Simpson devised a plan to fulfill his personal desire without his parents' permission. He disregarded their values, defied their authority and secretly went about doing what he knew he was forbidden to do.

Simpson's own recollection of the incident reveals the inherent connection between parental authority and spiritual rebellion against God's authority in his life.

> My first definite religious crisis came at about age fourteen. Prior to this I had earnestly desired to study for the ministry. . . . My carnal heart rebelled against the ministry because of the restraints it would put upon me . . . and for a time my . . . soul raged a battle over this.[3]

Young Simpson disregarded his parents' authority and will and began walking away from the possibility of ministry by pursuing something he believed pastors could not do. For a time it was an exhilarating experience. He was having the time of his life until his mother discovered what he was doing.

> It was the day of judgment for me . . . my mother wringing her hands and pouring out the vials of her wrath while I sat confounded and crushed. . . . That tragedy settled the question of the ministry. Soon after I . . . decided to give up these side issues and prepare myself . . . to be a minister of the Gospel.[4]

Simpson's response to his parents' authority became the occasion for settling the issue of his submission to Christ's authority, call and leading in his life. The incident was not trivial or inconsequential. It was a defining moment that established the place of submission in Simpson's life with Christ. As this place and role continued growing, Simpson decided to express his devotion to Christ's authority in writing:

> I bow in submission before Thee. . . . Thou hast subdued my rebellious heart by Thy love. So now take and use it for Thy glory. Whatever rebellious thoughts may arise therein . . . overcome them and bring into subjection everything that opposeth itself to Thy authority. I yield myself unto Thee as one alive from the dead, for time and eternity. Take me and use me entirely for Thy glory. . . . I am now a soldier of the Cross and a follower of the Lamb, and my

> motto henceforth is, "I have one King, even Jesus." . . . Place me in
> what circumstances Thou mayest desire.[5]

This initial step established the place of Christ's authority within
Simpson's soul. His heart was poised to follow the Lord's leading.
The journey into a life of surrender and submission was beginning.

To those who are apprehensive of or reluctant to surrender,
Simpson offered reassuring words:

> We are safe in this abandonment. . . . [W]e are not falling over a
> precipice or surrendering ourselves to the hands of a judge, but
> that we are sinking into a Father's arms and stepping into an in-
> finite inheritance.[6]

As a result our spiritual senses become "the organs of God's operation. . . . [We are] made alive by His own quickening life within
us."[7]

Knowing and understanding this, Simpson challenged us to
yield ourselves to Christ and to live in submission to the Lord:

> [We] must step down into the death of all of our strength and all
> our life, and surrendering ourselves completely to Him, rise in
> newness of life with Christ, and thus receive the Holy Spirit as
> the seal and source of that new life.[8]

> So we are to look upon the present life with all of its darkness
> and perplexity as only the soil of the future, casting it into the
> seed of faith, stepping out on the promises of God, trusting our
> souls to His keeping, and yielding our lives to His command.[9]

SUBMISSION PRODUCES ONENESS

As we move deeper into the discipline of submission, we are
drawing closer to Jesus. Our union with Christ increases in intimacy as our oneness with Him becomes greater than we ever
imagined possible. Jesus will impart His nature into us and make
it a second nature in our hearts, spontaneous in our choices and
victorious in our will.[10] He will cleanse us and share His life with
us in such a way that we will know that it is a life that does not
belong to us, but to Him.[11] Jesus "is the substance and supply of
our new spiritual life and fills us with His own Spirit and holiness. . . . We are a capacity; He is the supply."[12]

The capacity to receive and be filled with an even greater measure of Christ enlarges as we yield ourselves to Him. The surrendered life is tied to growth and maturity. Simpson likened it to the waves filling a pool. The waves sweep in from the sea and fill the little pool to its capacity. As a wave enters the pool, it enlarges it, and the next wave leaves an even deeper fullness than the one before.[13]

This illustration underscores the progressive nature of our spiritual development. Submission, surrender and yielding to Christ are ongoing qualities of the life that is consecrated to Jesus. For Simpson, the defining moment came while reading *The Higher Christian Life* by William Boardman. All of the experiences of Simpson's life and walk with Christ were preparing and leading him to that moment. The Spirit orchestrated all of the events to bring Christ's servant to the point where his eyes and mind would see the truth in a way that he had never experienced before.

> He saw the Lord Jesus revealed as a living, bright reality, as one who offered His own all-sufficient presence. Christ had not saved him merely from future peril and then left him to fight the battle of life, but the Christ who had justified him was waiting to sanctify him. Through the Holy Spirit, Christ had come to enter his spirit and to substitute His strength, holiness, joy, love, faith, and power for the helplessness and emptiness that had so troubled him. As Simpson threw himself at the feet of such a glorious Master, he claimed the promise, "I will dwell in you and walk in you." Across the threshold of his heart came a presence as real as the Christ who had come to John on Patmos. "From that moment," asserted Simpson, "a new secret [became] the charm, glory, and strength of his life and testimony."[14]

While the consecration may take place in one great comprehensive act of submission and dedication to Jesus, there are many subsequent acts of submission to Christ. Simpson viewed these as natural developments that characterize a life that is growing in the grace of Jesus Christ.

> [A]s new light comes to us and we become conscious of new powers or possibilities we can lay at His feet, to say our glad yes

to His claim as often as it is renewed. This is only the working out
in detail of the all-inclusive consecration that we made at first.[15]

Submission to Christ's leading characterized the transitions involved in Simpson's ministry. The vision burning within Simpson's
soul included new dimensions of ministry and expanding avenues
of opportunity for Christ's kingdom that could only be realized by
moving to places where they could become a reality.

The conclusion of Simpson's pastoral ministry in Hamilton, Ontario, was accompanied by two growing realizations. First, the outward growth of the Knox Presbyterian Church had reached its
maximum under his pastoral leadership. Any future evangelistic
potential was overshadowed by the need to build up those who,
through his ministry, came to Christ and into the fellowship of the
church.[16] Simpson's evangelistic fervor, coupled with his growing
passion for the lost, made him more naturally inclined to give himself to working in the harvest field rather than to the ongoing process involved in discipleship and nurturing ministries.

Second, the seeds of a new vision offering the opportunity for an
expanded ministry for Christ were planted within his heart
through his participation in the Evangelical Alliance conference in
New York City during the fall of 1873. Simpson's acquaintance
with the Evangelical Alliance and the unexpected opportunities
that came his way during the conference caused Simpson to begin
thinking about what could be accomplished for Christ through interdenominational cooperation on a global scale. During the conference, S.D. Burchard, pastor of New York's Thirteenth Street
Presbyterian Church, invited Simpson to bring a message to the
Thirteenth Street congregation. Seated in the sanctuary during
Simpson's message were members of the Louisville, Kentucky,
Chestnut Street Presbyterian Church. At the conclusion of the service they approached Simpson and invited him to consider coming
to Louisville. Simpson must have sensed that the Lord was opening
a new door of opportunity, for as soon as the conference was over
he went to Louisville to meet the people and to satisfy himself by
personal acquaintance with the situation.[17]

As Simpson considered these developments, the Spirit used
the vision growing within his heart to release him from the call to

serve a congregation and a community he loved to enter a new field of opportunity for Christ's kingdom. Although members of his congregation praised Simpson's ministry and expressed the hope that he would remain their pastor,[18] Simpson submitted to the Lord's leading in his life and accepted the call to a new place of service and opportunity for Christ in Louisville.

In Louisville, Simpson discovered a willingness to embrace the interdenominational cooperation that characterized the Evangelical Alliance. Denominational affiliations and identity were set aside for a greater good. Uniting a city wounded and torn apart by the bitterness and strife the Civil War had caused was paramount to Simpson and other leaders who prayed and worked for the healing of their community. Reconciliation and harmony between believers could only please the Lord and serve as a vital element in the process of reaching people for Jesus Christ. Simpson delighted in his congregation's eagerness to take the message of Christ's love out into the streets, to places where people who needed the Lord were comfortable in gathering. Evening services in the church gave way to special outreach ministries in theaters and other places.

As Simpson considered what God was doing, he sensed the Lord giving him a new vision for ministry. The ends of the earth and the unreached people of the world began playing an increasingly vital role in his thinking. The burden of his heart was growing larger and expanding beyond the ability of any single congregation's field of ministry. Simpson led his congregation in establishing and centering their evangelistic efforts on Louisville's unchurched community.

The focusing of Simpson's ministry there was the catalyst the Lord would use in placing on Simpson's heart the greatest concentration of unreached people in the nation. Even as he worked and served in Louisville, the Spirit was moving Simpson's heart toward the unreached people streaming into America through New York City. This influx of people represented the greatest field of opportunity to influence and win the unreached to Jesus Christ that Simpson had ever known.

Even as the outreach ministries in Louisville began to take off, Simpson felt that he was being led elsewhere. He was offered the pastorate of the Thirteenth Street Presbyterian Church, and he felt that the Lord was directing him to take it. This time, living in submission to Christ's authority would mean moving at a time and to a place his wife was apprehensive about and reluctant to embrace.

Simpson continued to strive for complete submission to Christ's will in his life. Subsequently, his submission to what Christ was accomplishing within his heart would prompt him to resign the pastorate of the Thirteenth Street Presbyterian Church in New York City within a few years of assuming pastoral leadership of that congregation. His short time there was all that it took for his heart to grow in its love and desire to reach people for Christ—particularly those people whom the members of his congregation were unwilling to embrace, let alone accept into Christian fellowship. Simpson had no choice but to follow where the Lord was leading even though he did not know where the journey would end or how God would provide along the way.

Spiritual growth and maturity bring with it the ongoing realization of new things and areas of life to surrender to the Lord. Surrendering them is exactly what A.B. Simpson did as he continually embraced the discipline of submission.

SUBMITTING BY DEGREES

There is also the opportunity to consecrate the individual members of our bodies to the Lord. The dynamics that are involved in this entail a deeper level of scrutiny and closer examination than a broad, sweeping surrender of the life to Christ. Presenting each individual member to Christ affords us the opportunity to discover hidden or secret pockets of resistance. We may find areas of our lives that we are reluctant to surrender and give over to the Lord. It is as though they have a mind and a will of their own. They are unwilling to submit to the authority of Christ. The Apostle Paul mentions the internal conflict that waged within his own life. Within his heart and mind he delighted in God's law. He wanted to live in obedience to Christ. But another law was working in the members of his body, seeking things that were contrary to the desire of his heart (see Romans 7:21-23). The same type of conflict can occur within our lives as well.

Simpson discovered this conflict arising within his own life as he sought to advance the cause of Christ. He faced a dilemma. Financial resources were needed to care for his family and to fund the independent ministry he had launched after resigning his pastoral position. With the needs of his family pressing in upon him, Simpson wondered how to fund the "work." Then he made what seemed to be a reasonable decision. By making freelance submissions to various literary magazines, Simpson could generate enough funds to care for his family and provide resources for his fledgling ministry.

The motive was pure and the objective faultless. But it was not the Lord's way. The Spirit checked Simpson's heart.[19] Although he did not know how God was going to supply, Simpson yielded to the Spirit's prompting.

Submitting to Christ's authority involves all aspects of our lives, including the members of our bodies. The pressure to meet the mounting needs of the moment could cause some to act in a well-intentioned way that is contrary to what God intends and will bring to pass if we will trust and obey.

This is why Simpson encouraged us to bring every member of our bodies to Christ, submitting and dedicating each part of our bodies to the Lord. "It adds great force and definiteness to it to make it explicit and to recognize every individual member as particularly yielded to His ownership and control."[20] He also noted that:

> God allows things that are lurking in our nature to assert themselves in order to reveal to us these hidden sources of danger and bring to an issue a conflict which deepens our spiritual life and leads to the uprooting and destroying of hidden sins. Thus God will bring to light, as we are able to bear it, all the things in our spiritual life that need to be discovered and destroyed, and we shall learn to thank Him for each new conflict because it assures a deeper life and a more complete deliverance from all the power of evil.[21]

In this regard Simpson warned us about the danger the senses pose to spiritual vitality. "Nothing so easily sets us wandering out into dangerous fields and by-path meadows as the senses of the body."[22] Consequently, he asked, "Is not this the real source of most of our difficulties about a holy life? We allow the unholy world to sweep in through all the avenues of our beings and absorb all our attention until there is inevitable pollution and misery."[23]

To guide us through the process of presenting and submitting the members of our bodies to Christ, Simpson posed some forceful questions for our consideration.

> Are the faculties of understanding dedicated [to God]? . . . Is our intelligence devoted to know His Word and will, and to "consider everything a loss compared to the surpassing greatness of knowing Christ Jesus my Lord?" (Philippians 3:8). Is our memory dedicated to be stored with His truth? Does our imagination dwell upon His Word until it makes the things of eternity more real and vivid than the objects of the senses? . . .
>
> Is our understanding and intellect filled with God? He must possess us Himself and put in us His thought and mind as well as His spirit and grace. The Christ who came to give Himself to us had not only a divine nature but a reasonable soul. This He imparts to us in union with His person.[24]

These questions force us to face issues that could be inadvertently overlooked. They challenge us to make a hard examination of our lives and truthfully determine if we have really submitted and dedicated every facet and dimension of our beings to Jesus Christ.

Periodically Simpson stepped aside from his personal and ministerial responsibilities for a time of reflection and self-examination of his commitment to Christ. It was also a time for the Spirit to search his heart, mind, soul and spirit. Simpson waited upon the Lord to bring to light anything that needing to be resolved and addressed in his relationship with Christ. On two separate occasions—September 1, 1863, and April 18, 1878—Simpson sensed it was appropriate to re-sign and date *A Solemn Covenant: The Dedication of Myself to God* (Appendix A), indicating his continuing submission and devotion to Jesus Christ. Brief statements written next to these dates affirmed Simpson's continuing devotion to the Lord. In doing so he recognized that there were moments when he had not met his ideals. Even more significant is the determination to own his shortcomings and continue reaching higher and moving forward in his life with Christ.[25]

The greater our level of submission to Jesus, the more we realize how much more there is to submit. The life of consecration is realized through continual submission to Christ. We enter into His life and also into His death. Simpson states:

> There is a sense in which we may die with Him to the power of sin in our lives. . . . There is a point where we definitely yield and accept Him. But this must be transacted in all the details of our actual life, as He meets us in His providence and brings us face-to-face with the very experiences which introduce us into actual fellowship with His earthly life, and enable us to live it over again with Him. . . . He does not expect from us either strength or goodness, but one to ignore our strength and goodness, and to take Him instead as our all sufficiency.[26]

Simpson's life, teaching and ministry challenge every Christian to settle the issue of Christ's authority by submitting and surrendering his life to Jesus.

> There must come a definite and entire surrender of your life to God . . . an act of consecration which will give to Him the right to take possession of you and work His gracious and perfect will in you and through you. God will not take you until you of your own volition give yourself up.[27]

This issue, like all other spiritual issues, is resolved through the working of the Spirit within us. The Christian life presents us with an endless succession of opportunities to work out and prove our submission to Christ's authority. Submission to the Lord is a continual process that unfolds with the passing of time. Each individual act of submission becomes the stepping-stone for the next. Each new revelation of light calls for new obedience and new advances in the life of Christ.

The call for submission and obedience may come in unexpected ways. Something that seems insignificant can become the occasion to affirm and prove our devotion to the Lord. Such an occasion came to Simpson while he was traveling in the Far East.

The testing came following a successful ministry in India. As he reflected on his time there, Simpson's heart was filled with praise and gratitude for what Christ had accomplished. As he was traveling to the next destination, he discovered that his luggage was missing. All his personal effects and the papers he needed were gone. The person entrusted with caring for Simpson's luggage had failed to fulfill his responsibility.

Naturally this discovery sparked frustration in Simpson. The carelessness was more than an inconvenience; it had the potential to disrupt, even hinder, the ministry awaiting Simpson at the next destination. This was Satan's moment to exploit this misfortune to his advantage. If he could discredit the messenger, the message would be discredited as well.

As Simpson thought about the difficulties that would come out of this carelessness and how it could adversely affect the Lord's work, he heard the sound of the Lord's voice speaking to his soul.

> Never will I forget how the Spirit met me with this question, "Are you going to fail in that which is more important than all your work, your own personal victory? Or are you going to trust Me and triumph through My grace and take all of this from My hand?" It was a keen but decisive struggle, and in a few minutes the Holy Spirit gave me strength to commit all to God and to go on my way in peace.[28]

Simpson settled the issue. The Lord is the Lord of all. Christ orchestrates life's circumstances and events, including careless misfortune, to accomplish God's purpose. In a matter of days the incident would become a source of encouragement to the missionaries awaiting his arrival. The Spirit used this incident to strengthen their faith and trust in the Father. The issues they struggled with were not mastering a foreign language or sharing the message, but the little insignificant things that Satan used to steal their joy. The story of Simpson's submission to Christ's authority in the inconvenient things enabled them to resolve issues they were dealing with in their own relationships with God.

Submission to Christ's authority must be resolved before personal agendas and the assertion of individual wills can give way to mutual submission within the Body of Christ. Those who have not resolved the issue of Christ's authority will experience recurring incidents of conflict in their spiritual journeys. The conflict will be in their own relationships with Christ, but it will not be confined to this isolated sphere. It will be manifested in their relationships with other people, especially those within the Body of Christ. Their lack of submission to the Lord will pose a hindrance to the advance of the gospel, for they will have difficulty submitting themselves to those who watch over their souls and who are entrusted with ministries of leadership within the Church.

The Church is commonly considered a volunteer organization. It is more than that, however; it is composed of people called of God and given a new identity through the regenerating work of the Holy Spirit. Believers are placed within the Body through the power of the Spirit. Each and every member is given at least one spiritual gift in accordance with the Spirit's desire, with the purpose of building up the Church. Christ's Body grows through the proper working and mutual submission of each part.

What may have been Simpson's most difficult act of mutual submission came in the twilight days of his life. He needed to be free of some outstanding financial indebtedness, so he agreed to let others help him resolve the financial issues. It was also time for Simpson to receive some compensation for his years of unpaid ministry and service to the missionary movement he had founded. He accepted a modest allowance to care for the needs of his household.[29]

In accepting assistance, Simpson demonstrated his submission to the Body of Christ in a sensitive personal matter. In doing so he affirmed the law of Christ: "By this all men will know that you are my disciples, if you love one another" (John 13:35). The fulfillment of our mutual responsibilities flows out of our love and submission to one another. This is grounded in our submission to the authority of Christ. In doing so we place Christ where others can see Him.

This is a primary objective of evangelization and sanctification, for it is as people see Jesus that they may place their hope and trust in Him. As we see Jesus we realize that we are set apart for His service and recognize that the Spirit is working to fashion us into His character. Simpson said, "My most important work has usually been to get myself and my shadow out of the people's way, and set Jesus fully in their view."[30]

Seeing Jesus—this was the ultimate objective of A.B. Simpson's life and ministry. It is an objective that could never have been realized or fulfilled apart from the discipline of submission. In submission the believer's life is separated from sin and dedicated to Jesus Christ. In submission we see the fullness of Jesus in ways we have never seen it before. When we are in submission, people see Jesus living in us in ways they have never seen Him before. If we follow Simpson's steps into complete and total submission to Christ, our lives will be hidden with Him. The only person other people will see is Jesus. This is what the world needs to see—Jesus Christ living in you and in me, the hope of glory (see Colossians 1:27).

In His Heart and Hand

In His heart my Saviour hides me,
And He holds me in His hand.
At His feet I sit and listen,
And I go at His command.

In His heart no ill can reach me;
In His hand no fear I know.
At His feet I love to linger,
At His call I love to go.

Keep me in Thy heart abiding,
Precious Brother, Bridegroom, Friend;
To Thy hands my all committing,
Guard and guide me to the end.[31]

CONSIDERATIONS FOR YOUR SPIRITUAL DEVELOPMENT

The ultimate example of submission is Jesus. Jesus submitted Himself to the will of the Father so that God's great redemptive purpose could be realized for mankind. Jesus said, "I have come down from heaven not to do my will but to do the will of him who sent me" (John 6:38). We are the beneficiaries of our Savior's submission. He was submissive unto death that culminated in life through the power of the resurrection.

Embracing the discipline of submission places us in a position to follow in the footsteps of Jesus Christ. It frees us from the tyranny of having to have our own way as we live under the authority of Jesus who loves us and died for us.

Submission is a concept that is foreign to the thinking of many. It shouldn't be, because everyone lives under and in submission to some authority, whether it is the authority of the government, the structure of a community, a social or civic organization, the rules of commerce or simply the authority of the home and family.

However, in the spiritual realm, when we submit to the authority of Christ we meet with formidable opposition from two sources. The first source, Satan, does not want us to submit to the Lordship of Jesus Christ. Satan knows that if he is successful in persuading us to desire to retain control, he will keep us from entering into the fullness of God's blessing in the life of Christ. He also realizes that the part we hold back is the pivotal foothold he can use to influence other areas of our lives. In addition to this, the Evil One recognizes that God's empowering for service can never be fully realized in the lives of those who hold part of their lives back.

The second source of opposition comes from the old man, the sinful nature that wages war against the things of the Spirit.

● ● ● ● ● ● ● ● ● ● ● *Application*

1. Describe how submission to Jesus is evident in your life.
2. How do you overcome the suggestion to hold back from Christ, to keep something in reserve?
3. The extent of our submission to Jesus can be seen in the submission we exhibit to the Body of Christ. Submission isn't an issue when people are in agreement. When there is disagreement, that is another story! People who insist on having their own ways have not entered into the submission of Christ. Can you recall a time when you practiced submission within the Body, the Church? What did God accomplish through it?

My Heart to His

Prayer as a Way of Life

The life of prayer was the foremost discipline of engagement in
A.B. Simpson's life and ministry. Prayer was such a dynamic
and indispensable element in his relationship with Christ
that others intuitively knew that his was a life of prayer. People acquainted with Simpson during his first pastorate sensed his devotion to prayer: "There was indeed 'a strong current of faith and
habit of prayer' within the young man which was recognized in the
Canada Presbyterian Church by friends, teachers, clergy, and laity
alike."[1] This habit of prayer did not diminish with the passing of
time—it intensified. Looking back and reflecting on the life of his
friend, Kenneth Mackenzie commented: "He was a man of prayer.
One need not expand that fact, but to testify of him that it was his
'vital breath, his native air.' "[2]

The vision for the work Christ was calling him to accomplish
was impressed upon Simpson's soul through prayer. By waiting
upon the Lord he received the empowering needed to accomplish
Christ's vision. Prayer was the prevailing force that strengthened
his soul through times of intense spiritual conflict and difficulty.
Calling upon the Lord in prayer sustained Simpson's hope as the
"ministry of the night" encompassed him. In prayer he offered to
Christ, his Lord, all of the praise, thanksgiving and glory for the
things accomplished through the life they shared.

Parental Prayer Influence

Prayer's influence touched Simpson's life the moment he was
born. James and Jane Simpson dedicated their newborn son, Albert Benjamin, to Jesus Christ. In doing so they expressed the de-

sire to see God call their son into Christian ministry. The place and nature of his service to Christ were left to the Lord's sovereign wisdom. As parents they would do everything within their power to prepare the way for the moment when their son would commit his life to Jesus. They made their public expression of this commitment when they stood before the congregation to present their son to Christ in baptism. Holding the baby in his arms, John Geddie, Canada's first Presbyterian missionary, prayed that God would call Albert Benjamin Simpson to missionary service.

Twenty-one years later, Geddie returned to Canada from the South Sea Islands and visited the campus of Knox College. He met with an aspiring ministerial student who was anticipating graduation and the call to serve his first pastorate. There was something he needed to share with this student. In the conversation that followed, Geddie reminded A.B. Simpson of the prayer he had offered to the Lord at Simpson's baptism. Simpson needed to know that God's call upon his life to ministry was nothing less than the answer to the prayers consecrating him to Christ's service.[3]

The direction of Simpson's life, the path he was pursuing, must be understood for what it is—God's answer to prayer. In prayer the Simpsons had asked God to choose their son for service in Christian ministry. John Geddie's baptismal prayer consecrating Simpson to the Lord's service reaffirmed his parents' desire. Throughout the years James and Jane Simpson continually prayed for their son, committing and trusting his future to the Lord.

Simpson had many memories of his parents calling upon the Lord in prayer during his formative years. His parents introduced him to the discipline of prayer before he affirmed his own profession of faith in Jesus Christ. As a young boy he learned to talk with Jesus about everything, as if Jesus were there with him, listening to every word.

Simpson remembered his father as a man who began each day seeking the presence of the Lord. "I can still remember Dad getting up before dawn, reading his Bible by candlelight and lingering at his devotions. It filled my soul with a kind of sacred awe."[4] Simpson recalled slipping out of bed in the middle of the night to pray for his mother. "I still remember how I used to rise and kneel beside my little bed, even before I knew God for myself, and pray for Him to comfort her."[5] As a child, Simpson's actions attested to an underlying awareness of the importance of praying for others and of God's willingness to answer prayer.

His personal recollections included an illustration of God's answer to a boy's prayer:

> I had lost a boy's chief treasure, an old jackknife, with which I was playing, and I still remember an impulse came to me to kneel down and pray about it. Soon afterwards I was delighted to find it. The incident made a profound impression upon my young heart and gave me a lifelong conviction, which has since borne fruit many times, that it is our privilege to take everything to God in prayer. I do not mean to convey the idea that I was at this time truly converted. . . . I only knew God in a groping, faraway sense.[6]

Simpson affirmed the role prayer played in his own life while acknowledging the goodness of God toward one who had not yet committed his life to Christ. Answered prayer and the realization of God's concern for those who pray may persuade an individual to trust in the Lord. Simpson understood and explained this on the principle of faith.

> But I can see now that God was discounting my future and treating me in advance as if I were already His child, because He knew that I would come to Him later and accept Him as my personal Savior and Father. This perhaps explains why God does so many things in answer to prayer for persons who do not yet know Him fully. He is treating them on the principle of faith, and "calling the things that are not as though they were."[7]

These experiences exerted a positive formative influence upon Simpson. They affirmed the importance and value of prayer while favorably inclining his heart's affection to the role of prayer in his own spiritual development.

Once Simpson committed his life to Christ, everything became a matter of conversation with Jesus. Every development in the unfolding ministry Christ had entrusted to him flowed out of a vision born in prayer. Simpson continually talked to the Lord about the work they were doing together. Everything was a matter of conversation with the Father.

Unanswered Prayer

A.B. Simpson readily acknowledged that there are times when the Lord does not answer our prayers. The reasons may range from the simplistic to the complex. No matter what the reason, we may be assured of one undeniable fact: God's denial is an affirmation of Christ's love for us. There are times when the Lord's love for us and concern for our well-being causes Him to withhold or to deny our request.

> Many of the things we ask for in our blindness have serpents coiled in their folds, but He loves us too much to give us such an answer. Sometimes He must modify or refuse our petition if He would be our true Father.[8]

Knowing the hidden danger and the potential detriment granting the request could pose to the petitioner's spiritual vitality, to others or to the work of the gospel, the Lord graciously denies petitions that contain unseen dangers.

Simpson identified timing as an important factor in what may seem to be unanswered prayer. Some petitions are denied because the timing is not right. Unknown to us, but perceived and understood by God, there may be things concerning the circumstances, the situation, the work Christ is seeking to accomplish, other people and even ourselves that cause the Lord to deny the request because the timing is not right.

On many occasions Simpson found himself standing before open doors of opportunity that he believed represented the will of God only to see them close unexpectedly.

> [H]e was content to leave behind a cold, disappointing horizon, the most cherished desires, with the prayer, 'Lord, Thou knowest.' And so in light and darkness, he slowly built the immense fabric of his heart's longing by simply doing the next thing and waiting for light and liberty.[9]

Simpson understood the vital role timing plays in the kingdom of God. Granting a request at the wrong or inappropriate time could hinder the cause of Christ or impede the gospel's advance. He was willing to accept and abide by the Spirit's leading, confident in the Lord's wisdom and knowledge of all things.

> Things that God in other circumstances would be quite willing to give us, He often has to refuse us because they would separate us from Him. At a later period in our lives, we find Him able and willing to give us the same things without reserve, because in the meantime we have been able to lay them all on the altar to be used for His glory and in union with Himself.[10]

Simpson noted that there are times when we are not personally or spiritually ready to receive what we have requested. There are things that Christ must first accomplish within our lives before the interior life is positioned to receive the answer to our prayers. Granting the request prematurely could hinder one's relationship with God. Again we see God's grace and mercy displayed in ways that advance life in Christ by denying the petition brought before Him.

This recognition is something Simpson came to understand through his own experience.

> I wanted to write and speak for Christ and to have a ready memory, so as to have the little knowledge I had gained always under command. I went to Christ about it and asked if He had anything for me in this way. He replied, "Yes, my child, I am made unto you Wisdom." . . . He said that He would be my wisdom. . . . He could cast down imaginations and bring into captivity every thought to the obedience of Christ that He could make the brain and the head right, then I took Him for all that.[11]

The motive was good. There is nothing wrong with wanting to be an effective communicator for Jesus Christ. Simpson recognized his weakness and made this the subject of his prayer request. He wanted Christ to grant him the ability to be able to recall everything he had learned at will.

However, this was not what A.B. Simpson needed to be an effective communicator for Christ. What he needed was the wisdom and the mind of Christ. Instead of being in control of his knowledge, he needed something more: He needed Christ to be in control of his knowledge, thoughts, emotions and intellectual processes. He also needed Christ to be in control of his heart. He needed the Lord's transforming touch upon his mind and within his heart. In

declining Simpson's request, Christ gave Simpson what he really
needed, and that was far more than he ever imagined or asked for.

Some unanswered prayers must be seen and understood for
what they really are—expressions of God's grace, mercy and lov-
ingkindness to those who believe. Other unanswered prayers must
be understood for what they are—the evidence of life and relationship with Christ that are not what they should be. The silence of
God to our petitions serves to remind us to look at our hearts and
examine our lives. Knowingly or unknowingly, could we be harboring something within our lives, in our relationships with other people or in our relationships with God that hinders our prayers? There
is a possibility that we ourselves are both the cause and the reason
for unanswered prayers. If this is the case, let us have the courage to
examine ourselves so that we can know what it is, so the issue may
be resolved, things made right and our life in Christ be characterized by oneness and harmony.

There are some instances in which we can take the steps that are
necessary to remove the hindrances to prayer. The place to begin is
by recognizing the obstacles for what they are—impediments to
the life in Christ and deterrents to the fulfillment of God's purpose
within the world. A.B. Simpson identified several contributing factors to unanswered prayer in a series of messages that was later
published as the book *The Life of Prayer*.

Simpson challenges us to examine our hearts, our relationships
with the Lord and with others, so we may discern the presence of
unconfessed sin in our lives. The psalmist's declaration, "If I had
cherished sin in my heart,/ the Lord would not have listened;/ but
God has surely listened/ and heard my voice in prayer./ Praise be to
God,/ who has not rejected my prayer/ or withheld his love from
me!" (Psalm 66:18-20), must not be denied. Confession opens the
pathway of communication with God. Conversely, consciously harboring sin effectively interferes with the process. Simpson main-
tained that God hears the prayers of sinners, but notes that this is a
totally different issue from expecting God to answer our prayers
"when we are deliberately committing sin."[12]

We are challenged to examine our lives and deal with the issues
so that our prayers, relationships with God and even our relation-

ships with other people are unhindered. This examination is in response to God's efforts to reconcile a relationship marred by sin. David's confession came after a long period of cover-up and denial and at the expense of peace within his soul. The inner turmoil he experienced must be understood as a demonstration of God's reconciling grace seeking a restoration of life and fellowship with Him.

David describes his torment in Psalm 32 and Psalm 38:

> When I kept silent,
>   my bones wasted away. . . .
> For day and night
>   your hand was heavy upon me;
> my strength was sapped. (Psalm 32:3-4)
>
> For your arrows have pierced me,
>   and your hand has come down upon me.
> Because of your wrath there is no health in my body;
>   my bones have no soundness because of my sin.
> My guilt has overwhelmed me
>   like a burden too heavy to bear.
> My wounds fester and are loathsome
>   because of my sinful folly.
> I am bowed down and brought very low;
>   all day long I go about mourning.
> My back is filled with searing pain;
>   there is no health in my body.
> I am feeble and utterly crushed;
>   I groan in anguish of heart. . . .
> My heart pounds, my strength fails me;
>   even the light has gone from my eyes. (38:2-8, 10)

The cost of unconfessed sin includes physical, emotional, intellectual, social and spiritual considerations, in addition to unanswered prayers. May we understand the consequences of sin as an appeal from God's reconciling mercy, imploring us to confess the sin and restore fellowship with Jesus Christ.

Simpson also identified several underlying considerations that may be contributing factors to unanswered prayer. He noted that a lack of trust frequently results in our own restless activity or flight that hinders God's answer to our requests. Instead of waiting upon the Lord, there is a tendency to become impatient with the passing of time. So we involve ourselves in doing the things we think are necessary to bring about the answer to our prayers.[13] This is not trust. It is trying to force or manipulate the answer by our own means instead of waiting upon God. The reasonable, rational, logical thing to do may be nothing less than a mirrored reflection of Sarai's plan to have a child through Hagar (see Genesis 16). We have to trust the Lord and wait until He brings the answer to us and works it out in our lives. Without this we are sure to do something to hinder things or to get ourselves in a place where we cannot receive the answer in its fullness.[14]

A lack of trust must not be interpreted as doubt. Simpson felt that there was a distinctive, qualitative difference between a lack of trust and doubt. Those with a lack of trust are convinced God can do what they ask. They believe it is possible; they are just not sure that God will accomplish it for them or in the time they sense it has to be done. Doubt is altogether different. Those who doubt hesitate to believe that it is possible. They will ask; the concern will be a matter of prayer. But it is a prayer void of confidence or faith that God will answer. It questions the veracity of God's character, promises and commitment to those who believe.

Consequently, Simpson saw the Adversary playing a role in seeking to engender doubt. The insinuation that God cannot be trusted was a pivotal element in Satan's strategy toward Eve. "Did God really say" (Genesis 3:1) was intended to breed doubt within Eve's mind. Simpson asserted that there is something we can do to guard against Satan's ploy: "We can refuse to doubt! We can refuse to entertain the questioning and fear, the morbid apprehension and subtle satanic insinuations."[15] Those who do so will see and know God's faithfulness in answered prayer.

Selfishness, a spirit of bitterness and strife, indiscriminate asking and unresponsiveness to the Spirit's leading are some of the other underlying considerations Simpson cited as possible reasons for unanswered prayer. Selfishness uses prayer as a means to fulfill personal desires and objectives instead of, and sometimes at the expense of, the redemptive work of Christ. When a spirit of bitterness and strife exists within a person's heart, whatever the reason, there is a disruption of the oneness and harmony Jesus seeks for the Body of Christ. This poses an impediment to effective intercession. A heart that refuses to respond to the Spirit's leading or direction is not living in submission to the Lordship of Jesus Christ. Stubbornness and self-will are detrimental to an effective prayer life. Without diminishing the importance of these and other factors, Simpson maintains that ignorance respecting the Holy Spirit and the interior life is the single prevailing factor posing the greatest hindrance to the life of prayer.[16]

Too many Christians fail to realize that prayer is far more than a religious activity. Interceding for others—presenting needs, petitions and requests to God in true prayer—flows out of a life lived in harmony with God.

> The life of prayer is an interior life, a spiritual life. Many people do not realize this and many actually do not want it. It holds too constant a check upon the heart. It requires too completely that they should walk with God. People like to be their own masters. The habit of walking step by step with God, submitting every thought and desire to an inward Monitor is intolerable to their imperious will. At the least it is unfamiliar to their experience.
>
> But this is truly the key to the life of prayer. It is an interior life.[17]

A.B. Simpson was convinced that a lack of understanding regarding the interior life is the primary hindrance to prayer. Many do not know that prayer is the natural expression of two hearts living in communion with one another as they seek the fulfillment of God's kingdom. Instead of intimacy with Christ, they settle for the outward form of religious conversation in the name of God.

A life of continuous submission to Christ, the sanctified life, a life devoted to God and set apart for the Lord's service, is crucial to experiencing, knowing and having effectiveness in intercession. To abide in Christ, "we must cultivate the habit of internal prayer, communing with God in the heart."[18] These essential elements are intricately interwoven and indispensable to both the Christ-life and the life of prayer. It is impossible to have one without the other.

TRUE PRAYER

The model that best illustrates the interior life of submission to Christ and communion with God is the Lord's Prayer. It is here that Simpson finds the key elements of true prayer. The first purpose of true prayer is the worship, adoration and glorification of God. We must "first become satisfied with God Himself and realize that His glory is above all our desires and interests."[19] God's identity, majesty and greatness form the prism of true prayer. As we see the Lord, we are positioned to pray according to the mind of Christ and the Spirit's leading.

This inevitably focuses upon the redemptive work of Christ and the continued expansion of God's kingdom in the power of the Spirit through the ministry of the Church of Jesus Christ. It "recognizes the establishment of the kingdom of God as the chief purpose of the divine will and the supreme desire of every true Christian."[20] True prayer must of necessity encompass every facet and dimension of the work involved with taking the gospel of salvation to the unreached people of the world.

Simpson believed that "prayer is the highest of all spiritual forces."[21] He was convinced that prayer would open the doors and provide the resources needed to seize opportunities for advancing the gospel of Christ.

> Let each of us give ourselves to this ministry to prayer as we never have before. Let us be definite and special; let us have our hour of missionary prayer and let nothing interrupt it. Let us have special ones for whom we pray, and yet not to forget to pray at all. Let us pray believing that we receive the things we ask for, and we shall then see the salvation of our God covering the earth and bending the heavens to meet the earth in the blessed coming of the Lord.[22]

This is prayer for the fulfillment of God's redemptive purpose in Christ Jesus. It is to the risen Christ that we must make our intercession and petitions known. Simpson notes that Christ wants us to turn our faces directly to Him. The attitude of prayer looks directly into the face of God with "unveiled countenance and loving, wholehearted confidence."[23]

Simpson saw the ancient incense altar as a foreshadowing of true prayer. It was a visual portrayal of hearts knitted together in love and devotion, desiring to honor and glorify God.

> The ascending incense continually filling the sacred chamber was the type of Christ. His whole being was one breath of love, sweetness and consecration to God, as well as a remembrance of us. . . . And, expressive of His intercession, the altar of incense fittingly becomes the example for our imitation and the pattern of our prayer, of our communion with God. It is a pattern of that sacred place where "spirits blend, and friend holds fellowship with friend."[24]

True prayer also anticipates and longs for the complete sanctification of God's people. It embraces the renunciation of our own will so we may desire and receive God's will instead. Once we recognize God's will "as the standard of our desires and petitions, we are to claim these petitions that are in accordance with His will, with a force and tenacity as great as the will of God itself!"[25] This is possible as we "come in His will and spirit, and ask what He Himself would ask."[26] True prayer never requests something that Christ would not ask for if He were praying. It petitions and intercedes in harmony with Christ's will through the leading of the Holy Spirit. These requests are made in the fullest confidence that God will hear and answer the prayer. For they are based and grounded on the finished work of Christ and our redemption privileges through His death and atonement.[27] It is asking for that for which Jesus suffered and died, and freely and fully purchased for all those who believe upon the name of Christ.[28]

Simpson is calling us to a level of prayer that is richer, fuller and deeper than many have ever known or imagined possible. True prayer is always conscious of God's mercy and redeeming grace. It flows out of a oneness with Christ, seeking the complete and total fulfillment of Christ's purpose within our own lives and for the people of the earth, even the ends of the earth, through the working of the Holy Spirit. This "spirit of prayer must be born from above and it cannot be imitated or counterfeited by mere human effort."[29] True prayer is nothing less than the mind of Christ expressed in the believer's petition to God. It is impossible to have true prayer without oneness with Christ.

Oneness with Jesus and oneness within the Body of Christ are primary expressions of the Lord's desire and intercession on behalf of those who believe in Him (see John 17). This oneness is brought about through God's sovereign working on our behalf. It is impossible to achieve oneness on our own. The protective power of God's name is crucial to achieving this oneness. "Holy Father, protect them by the power of your name—the name you gave me—so that they may be one as we are one" (17:11).

It also involves the intercession of Jesus for His own. "I pray . . . that all of them may be one, Father, just as you are in me and I am in you. May they also be in us so that the world may believe that you have sent me" (17:20-21). There is a third heavenly element involved in achieving the oneness Christ desires for His children. Added to the protective power of the Father's name and the intercession of Jesus is the glory the Father gave to the Son.

> I have given them the glory that you gave me, that they may be one as we are one: I in them and you in me. May they be brought to complete unity to let the world know that you sent me and have loved them even as you have loved me. (17:22-23)

Christ Jesus has given His glory to His own in order for the oneness that He is praying for to become a reality in their lives, relationships and experiences. This visible oneness has the power to influence lives and enhance the possibility of people coming to faith, repentance, salvation, forgiveness and life through Jesus Christ. The oneness that Christ prays for His Church is essential in missions and evangelism: The response of those who live in darkness hinges upon our oneness with the Lord and one another. Simpson understood this, modeled it, longed for it to be a distinguishing characteristic of Christ's community and joined his heart with Jesus in praying that it would be so.

Simpson lived to make Christ known to people who had never heard the name of Jesus. If this meant leaving areas where a witness for Christ had been established and the church planted to labor in other harvest fields, he was willing to do it. The prayer of his heart was for the Lord to show him the "pioneer fields."[30]

Oneness with Christ means that we are abiding in Him. Abiding in Jesus involves a life of continual trust and submission to the Lord. It exhibits the confidence the Apostle Paul expressed: "And we know that in all things God works for the good of those who love him, who have been called according to his purpose" (Romans 8:28). Even though we may not understand what is taking place or the reasons why it is happening, and though we may wrestle with circumstances that defy our hope in Christ, there is the sure and undeniable certainty that God is working to accomplish something good on our behalf. Simpson states,

> If we would abide in Christ we must remember that Christ has undertaken not only the emergencies of life, but everything; and so we must cultivate the habit of constant dependence on Him; falling back on Him and finding Him everywhere; recognizing that He has undertaken the business of our life, and there is not a difficulty that comes up, but He will carry us through if we let Him have His way, and just trust Him.[31]

As we do so and lift our voices to the Lord in prayer, we will discover that "[t]here is no blessing so great as that which comes when our hearts are lifted out of ourselves and become one with Christ in intercession for others and His cause."[32] The ministry of intercession, praying for others, is what Simpson considers the highest ministry of prayer.[33] As we enter into this ministry, we must do so realizing

> . . . there are some things we do not know. . . . [T]here are the divine things like the unknown spice. We cannot measure their depth or height.
>
> In our prayers there are things . . . we do not know. There ought always to be definiteness in our prayers. Often we may know what is according to His will and expect it. But perhaps the largest part of our praying in the Holy Spirit will be like the three unknown spices: we cannot tell just what the cry means. But we shall be conscious of the cry that cannot be articulated. We shall feel that God knows it. It is articulated in His ear and He will give us the answer and show us in due time.

> This may help you to understand many of your perplexing bur-
> dens of prayer. . . . There has been that unutterable outreaching
> that seemed incapable of interpretation or understanding—a
> prayer you did not comprehend and did not need to know.[34]

There are mysteries in prayer, mysteries that remain hidden and
unknown to us but are known to the Spirit. "The Spirit himself intercedes for us with groans that words cannot express . . . in accordance with God's will" (Romans 8:26-27). Abiding in Christ
unleashes the spirit of true prayer as the Spirit prays and intercedes
through us so Christ can be glorified as the Father's good and perfect purpose is accomplished. Knowing that the Spirit intercedes
according to God's will was all that Simpson needed to continue
abiding in Christ no matter what the circumstances were.
Simpson's diary reveals the joy of the blessing that belongs to those
whose hearts are knit together with Christ. "He has left nothing out
and nothing has failed of all His words and I have desired to give
myself ever and wholly a living and joyful sacrifice to Him in all
things."[35]

These words reveal Simpson's consecration to Jesus. Nothing
is held back. His life is a living sacrifice to the Lord. The intercession and prayer that flow from his heart are not his alone; they
are the prayer life he shares with the Spirit.

> In the consecrated believer the Holy Spirit is preeminently a
> Spirit of prayer. If our whole being is committed to Him and our
> thoughts are under His control, He will occupy every moment in
> communion. We shall bring everything to Him as it comes, and
> pray it out in our spiritual consciousness before we act it out in
> our lives. We shall, therefore, find ourselves taking up the bur-
> dens of life and praying them out in a wordless prayer which we
> ourselves often cannot understand, but which is simply the un-
> folding of His thought and will within us. This will be followed
> by the unfolding of His providence concerning us.[36]

Out of this abiding life with Christ there is still another dimension of prayer that is deeper than what Simpson has just described. It is the deepest level of prayer Simpson ever knew or
experienced: the contemplative life of prayer. He invites us to follow him into this life.

CONTEMPLATIVE PRAYER

In contemplative prayer, the discipline of prayer joins with the disciplines of silence and solitude. Thinking ceases as the heart and mind wait in silence before God. As we do so, we will discover that the Lord is waiting in the depths of our souls to talk with us, but first we must learn to listen. The listening dimension of prayer is the spirit's deepest need. In contemplative prayer we begin to know God in a new way and receive spiritual refreshing for our lives with Christ.[37] His presence permeates every aspect of our beings and we are strategically positioned to pray according to the will of God.

In contemplative prayer we are waiting upon God. Instead of seeking, we are receiving the favor of divine grace. The still, small voice of the Spirit speaks to the heart, mind and soul, revealing the mysteries of Christ that can only be heard by those who silently wait upon Him. In the midnight hour before Simpson was scheduled to preach the missionary message at Old Orchard, Mrs. May Agnew Stephens passed by Simpson's door and heard him softly saying, "Yes, Lord. Yes, Lord" over and over again.[38] Simpson was responding to the voice of the Spirit speaking to his heart. "There is a divine and most perfect provision in the economy of grace, by which the Holy Spirit adjusts our spirit into such harmony with God that we can catch His thought and send it back again, not merely as a human desire, but as divine prayer."[39] Surely this takes us into a facet of praying in the Spirit that is unknown to those who are too busy to enter into the silent waiting of contemplative prayer.

There is still an even deeper level of contemplative prayer. It is the most intimate prayer of all. Simpson says,

> It is often voiceless. It is communion. It does not ask for anything, but it just pours out its being in holy fellowship and silent communion with God. Sometimes it is an infinite rest to cease from all words and just lie still upon His. . . . There are moments too sacred, too divine for our interpretation. There are joys as well as groans which "cannot be uttered." . . . We should know the depths and heights of silent prayer and divine communion.[40]

Words do not have to be expressed to share life and love with each other. Silently being together, restfully enjoying the presence of God and savoring the sweetness of the other's presence is the deepest form of fellowship and communion that exemplifies the depths of abiding in Christ. It is to this level of intimacy with Jesus that Simpson summons us in the life of prayer. For it is here that we truly know the mind of the Lord and experience true oneness with the Son.

PERSONAL AND PASTORAL PRAYER LIFE

Every crucial decision in Simpson's life and ministry flowed out of his conversations with God. Prayer played a pivotal role in discerning Christ's direction for his personal life and ministry. Everything from everyday decisions to life-changing issues was a matter of prayer. William MacArthur states, "If God was his method of life, the same was true of his service. . . . I've heard him say, 'I am not good unless I can get alone with God.' "[41] Simpson recognized that there is more involved in prayer than making requests or presenting needs. Prayer is seeking the presence, mind and will of Christ. It is pressing into a fellowship, a communion with Him that carries with it every needed blessing.[42]

Nothing is too insignificant to bring to the Lord before making a decision. Simpson felt that those who neglect the habit of constant prayer in the momentary things of life will be unprepared to pray effectively in the times of unexpected emergencies.[43] The daily communion with the Lord prepares the way for drawing into the presence of Christ and discerning God's will in times of crisis or seasons of urgency.

Simpson made *A Solemn Covenant* at the end of a day set apart for seeking the Lord in fasting and prayer. The spiritual longing within his soul brought him to this moment of decision. Discerning Christ's will in the decision he was about to make concerning the rest of his life was essential. The circumstances and events leading up to that moment would not substitute for seeking the mind of Christ in fasting and prayer.

The place of prayer in Simpson's own life spilled over into his pastoral ministry. He sought to cultivate a higher level of prayer life in his first pastorate, Knox Church in Hamilton, Ontario.

> A great advance was made in the prayer life of the congregation by the institution of a social weekly prayer meeting in each elder's district, and later by establishing a united meeting for prayer at the close of the Wednesday evening lecture.[44]

Prayer played a formative role in deepening the spiritual vitality of the Knox Church congregation.

The scope and breadth of Simpson's intercession would soon reach beyond the congregational concerns associated with the regular work of the ministry to a city torn by bitterness and strife. Simpson assumed the responsibilities of his second pastorate, the Chestnut Presbyterian Church in Louisville, Kentucky, nearly a decade after the Civil War. The war was over, but the animosity and hatred spawned by slavery continued to divide the city. These attitudes had to fall before the reconciling love and peace of Jesus Christ.

Burdened for the spiritual condition of the city, Simpson devoted himself to extended periods of prayer and intercession. He called upon the Lord to break hardened hearts and bring revival to the Church that would convince the lost of their need for the Savior. Simpson invited the pastors of the city to a meeting to explore the possibility of sponsoring a cooperative evangelistic effort.

He recognized that revival would have to begin with the Spirit of the Lord breaking the hearts of the pastors. Simpson challenged them to set aside the differences that separated them and to seek the unity of the Lord. They went before the Lord on their knees in prayer. The Spirit of God came upon them, filling their hearts with His presence and love. This was the beginning of a revival in Louisville.[45]

It also was the beginning of a new work within Simpson's heart. God placed a burning desire upon his soul for the salvation of the lost. His prayers for a divided city soon gave way to intercession for the unreached masses. The work of prayer changed Simpson's heart. The Spirit was cultivating a vision for a global ministry within his soul. Simpson concluded that the place to begin casting the missionary vision was through the publication of a missionary magazine. Sensing the Spirit's leading to go ahead and begin working toward that goal, Simpson dedicated and committed the work to Christ in prayer.

> *I pray:*
> For wisdom and power for this work, as Pastor and Editor.
>
> For complete deliverance from the Power of Evil in my heart, home, and work in His way.
>
> For simple faith henceforth that He is doing all things well and I may be free from carefulness.
>
> For grace to walk in the Spirit wholly, always yielded to His will, trusting perfectly, triumphing over all sin and doubt and pleasing my Father *blamelessly.*
>
> For perfect freedom and simplicity in my feelings, and perfect independence in God and for Christ above all men.
>
> For a Christian temper and attitude toward my wife in everything, so as to fully please God and never regret a word, act or thought.
>
> For grace *in everything* to give thanks.[46]

Simpson's words reveal the desire to glorify Jesus Christ, not only in the publication of the magazine, but in his pastoral responsibilities and personal life as a husband and father. He recognized the danger Satan posed and sought divine protection from the Enemy.

An unprecedented season of intense conflict developed within the home over his emerging burden to take the message of salvation to the ends of the earth. Mrs. Simpson could sense her husband's desire for pastoral ministry giving way to a vision for unreached people. She understood his burden for Louisville, but it was difficult for her to comprehend his vision for the unreached people of the world. Mrs. Simpson did not yet share her husband's vision for a global ministry. Nor did she relish the possibility of leaving Louisville. Yet Simpson knew this spiritual conflict would ultimately be resolved through the faithfulness of God.

> I prayed and prayed for her until of late I cannot pray without intense distress. I leave her with Him trusting that He will lead her.

> . . . I wait in silence upon God. I trust that my own heart may be kept righteous, and merciful in everything.[47]

> Great trials today about Margaret. Led to continual prayer. Constant cloud and burden of pain. At times much sense of displeasure. I fear impatience of spirit. I pray to see God in it all. Much tenderness and love and hope today. Much peculiar sense of His Presence tonight. Praying much. May He give what He asks and I need.[48]

> Much solemn prayer and thought about my family. Able to pray for nothing else at times. Such elements of danger with work here—and us all. . . . Lord give Thy Mind ever. Help to leave all these cares on Thee—be independent of all natural feelings and filled with God.[49]

Simpson's intercession sought the Lord for the resolution of the issues troubling his wife while praying for the purity of his own heart's attitude and devotion to God. He did not want this conflict to become something that diminished his fellowship and communion with Christ. In God's time the issues within the Simpson household were resolved. Christ honored Simpson's intercession for his wife and the Spirit changed her heart. The conflict that threatened their relationship became the occasion to prove the faithfulness and the power of God.

Simpson's decision to accept the call to serve in New York City was forged in prayer. He could have cited a number of sound, rational reasons why such a move was advantageous. No one could argue against the logistical advantages New York City offered for realizing the missionary vision burning within his soul. However, these and other reasonable factors could not become a substitute for the one and only sufficient reason: the Lord's calling and leading. Simpson had to know that accepting the call to serve the Thirteenth Street congregation was at the center of God's will for his life and in the Lord's time. He sought resolution for all the questions surrounding the issue by going to the Lord in prayer.

> Peculiar burden tonight in Session meeting. My installation proposed and requested at an early day. Does the Master clearly bid this? Or does He hold me back at present and free me for a wider work—as I have often desired—as an Evangelist? Or does He bid

me receive this special charge at present and let Him open the way in the future for whatever else He may have? I will surely by His grace do whatever He shows. I want and must have His way and full blessing or I shall be unable to live.[50]

More than anything else, Simpson wanted a clear and certain confirmation that the decision he was about to make was in the center of Christ's will. If he followed his heart's inclination he would have moved into an evangelistic ministry. But this was neither the path nor the time for such an avenue of service for Christ. Jesus had something else in mind. The following day Simpson received the confirmation he was seeking. "God seemed to show today in answer to much prayer that it is His full will that I should press forward in this work. Also should be installed as soon as my letter comes."[51]

Simpson's pastoral ministry in New York City proved to be the necessary transitional step into a global ministry for the sake of the gospel. Immigrants seeking a new life in America filled the crowded streets of Manhattan. Simpson saw them as sheep without a shepherd. They were the unreached masses Christ came into the world to save. Simpson actively sought for ways to minister to the immigrants. Their response to the message of salvation fueled the passion burning in his soul.

As his burden for their salvation grew stronger, Simpson knew a decision would have to be made concerning the pastoral ministry. This decision could not be based upon circumstances, but in solitude before the Lord. At the end of a week devoted to seeking God in prayer, Simpson sensed the Spirit releasing him from the pastorate. This was the Lord's time to open the door of opportunity and grant His servant the freedom to pursue a ministry to the unreached masses of the world.[52] Prevailing prayer formed the foundation of this new work.

A little band of humble, praying Christians met in an upper room to begin this work for God, and we opened our Bibles, and these words were just before us: "Who hath despised the day of small things?"... We knelt before Him there and thanked Him that we were poor, that we were few, that we were weak, and threw ourselves upon the might of the Holy Ghost, and He has never failed us.[53]

Prayer was the founding, driving and sustaining force in the growth and development of the missionary society Simpson founded. Prevailing prayer overcame the obstacles encountered along the way. "We did not stop praying. . . . We prayed . . . and God stopped us from going too fast."[54] They came before the Lord in prayer, and God's Spirit honored the desires of their hearts. Every advance and initiative was bathed in prayer. "From the first . . . the highest aim of the Tabernacle has been to labor and pray to carry out the Great Commission."[55]

Simpson continually spoke to God about the things they were doing together. In prayer Simpson received a vision of what God wanted him to do. In conversation with the Father he discerned the steps to take in carrying out God's will. Through prayer he received the empowering of the Spirit to accomplish the task they were working on together. In answer to prayer God provided the resources that were needed to complete the task. With a heart filled with thanksgiving and praise, Simpson glorified the name of the Lord for the things they accomplished together.[56]

> This unbroken fellowship was maintained by definite communion and intercession. It was Dr. Simpson's habit to spend a time, after he had laid his work aside each night, in unhindered, conscious fellowship with Christ. He called it his love life, and it was as real to him as the interchange of thought and feeling between the most devoted lovers. It was his daily renewal of life, his rest before sleep, his outgiving of worship and adoration, and his inbreathing of the very fullness of God.[57]

The unfolding ministry of A.B. Simpson was born in a vision God gave to a man willing to seek the Father in prayer. As Simpson gave himself to fulfilling the vision, a passion burned within his soul. God was working within his life to plant the seeds of ministries greater than one man could accomplish in a lifetime. The twilight days of his life brought with them the growing realization that the work must be passed on to others. There was only one way for this to be done. It had to be given back as an offering to the Lord.

Simpson committed to the Lord the continuation of the vision, the work and ministry the Father had entrusted to him. Paul Rader expressed it in these words:

> He put out his arms and we knelt to pray. Oh, such a prayer! He started in thanksgiving for the early days, and swept the past in waves of praise at each step; then to the present; then on to the future—the prophet vision was marvelous. We were all with upturned, tear-stained faces praising God together with him as by faith we followed him to the mountain, and viewed the promised land. He was so sure that the Alliance was born in the heart of God. He lay there that night in a burst of praises, sure that God could carry it forward. He knew his physical life was closing. So reverently he lifted his hands as if passing the work over to God who had carried it all those days.[58]

Although the passing of time diminished Simpson's abilities, it did not hinder his communion and fellowship with God in prayer. "Though his grasp on the affairs of his life weakened, his sense of God's presence continued, and his last days were marked by spontaneous praise and intercession that were a benediction to all who were closely associated with him."[59] Spontaneous expressions of praise unto God coupled with petitions of intercession for the men and women engaged in the work of Christ among the unreached people of the world characterized the twilight days of Simpson's life. His life and ministry exemplify an unceasing commitment and devotion to the discipline of prayer. Prayer was more than the source of power and provision for the ministry of Christ. Prayer was the secret abiding place of the servant and the Master enjoying communion and fellowship with one another in the life and ministry they shared together.

CONSIDERATIONS FOR YOUR SPIRITUAL DEVELOPMENT

Prayer is an expression of trust in God concerning the life we share in Jesus and the work we are accomplishing together. It is grounded in the unshakable confidence of God's redeeming grace. Prayer is the intimate communion of two hearts knit together in love eagerly listening to hear what the other has to say. A quiet spirit patiently waiting to hear God's voice plays a vital role in cultivating a life of prayer. Quietly waiting to hear what God has to say to us is more important than anything we have to say.

Sometimes it seems as though people approach prayer with no intention of listening. Their prayer lists set the agenda. Once they are finished with their lists, the time of prayer is through. The communion of two hearts and lives is reduced to little more than a one-way conversation.

● ● ● ● ● ● ● ● ● ● ● *Application*

1. Think about your times of prayer. Do you set aside time to quietly wait and listen to hear the Lord's voice?
2. The life of prayer involves times when our prayers are not answered. Discuss or explain how unanswered prayer can be an affirmation of God's love for you. Share how unanswered prayer has kept you from dangers you did not anticipate or opened new doors of opportunity that you did not foresee.
3. In Psalm 66:18-20 David seems to affirm that harboring unconfessed sin in his life prevented God from hearing his prayer. Knowing the adverse affect this has, why would anyone permit something to reside in his heart that hinders his relationship with God? What are some of the things that keep people from dealing with their sin?
4. Identify other things that could be reasons for unanswered prayer.
5. Describe your ministry of intercession (praying for the members of your family, the people you are seeking to influence and win for Jesus Christ, the spiritual development of people within your church family, the ministry you are involved in, the ministries of your church, the advance of the gospel among the unreached people, etc.).
6. Identify some specific steps you can take to raise your prayer life to a higher level. What do you need to give up or let go of to improve your prayer life? What do you need to begin doing? If

you begin to embrace the spiritual discipline of prayer today, where do you think your prayer life will be six months or a year from now? What will God accomplish because you've prayed?

Disciplines
of Abstinence

Chapter
FOUR

GIVING YOUR LIFE AWAY
The Gift of *Sacrifice*

ugene Peterson compares spiritual disciplines to gardening tools that must be used properly with careful regard to the soil's condition and the needs of the plant.[1] We must become familiar with each of the tools, the disciplines, and be prepared to use them as they are needed. Developing competence in the proper use of the tools is essential to nurturing the spiritual life within. Some tools will be used once or twice a year. Others will be used far more frequently. Then there is the favorite tool, the tool that the gardener cannot do without. Time and time again the gardener relies on this one tool more than all of the rest. For this tool is indispensable in cultivating and nurturing a healthy, fruit-bearing plant.

The tool that A.B. Simpson reached for over and over again, the one tool that was absolutely essential in his spiritual formation and in furthering the ministry Christ entrusted to him, was the discipline named sacrifice. Simpson embraced sacrifice and never let it go. His life and ministry were characterized by sacrifice for the sake of knowing Christ and the pleasure of advancing the love and message of Jesus to unreached people at home and abroad.

Many Christians believe God wants to accomplish great things in the world. Some see a vision for what Christ longs to do in the hearts and lives of people living in darkness. Unfortunately, few—precious few—are willing to pay the price to move past familiar boundaries or comfortable surroundings for the sake of the gospel. Rare indeed are those who have the courage to make the sacrifices necessary to accomplish great things with the Lord.

Simpson achieved remarkable accomplishments for the Lord because he was willing to let the Spirit take his submission to Christ to a higher and deeper level. He moved beyond the realm of the necessary into a dimension of life with Christ that is unknown to many. His affection for Jesus did not stop with the things God expects or requires of His children. His devotion to the Savior was a relentless pursuit of the insatiable quest to find how much more he could offer to the Lord. Simpson's submission to Christ found its fullest expression in the sacrifices he continuously made in order to seize the moment for the sake of the gospel.

Christ used A.B. Simpson to advance the kingdom of God because Simpson was willing to pay the price. He intuitively understood that sacrifice is an ongoing process, not a one-time payment.[2] Advancing the cause of Christ requires new sacrifices each and every step of the way. Every new opportunity, every new advance of the gospel comes with a price. The sacrifices that have been made are down payments that qualify and position us to make the sacrifices that are necessary to continue advancing.

A.B. Simpson rejected the thinking that entices us to be content with what we have accomplished or achieved. These things are not ends in themselves. They are the foundation for the sacrifices that are necessary to reach deeper, higher and further for the Lord. He summons us to join him in the quest for and of the gospel: "Let us, then, be willing to be enlarged, although it may involve many a sacrifice, many a peril and many a hazardous undertaking."[3] There is a cost to be paid. Sacrifice upon sacrifice must be made to continue moving forward in the life of Christ. Simpson was willing to forsake everything in favor of trusting God. The discipline of sacrifice characterized his devotion to the Lord.

THE FOUNDATION FOR SACRIFICE

A.B. Simpson embraced sacrifice and made it a fundamental and indispensable discipline in his spiritual formation because he understood that the essence of the gospel is sacrifice. He was convinced that the sacrifice that characterized the Father and the Son should be abundantly evident in the lives of God's people.

> The law of sacrifice is the law of God. God who loved in supreme
> self-sufficiency as the Father, Son and Holy Ghost gave Himself.
> God's glory was in giving Himself. . . . The law of God is sacrifice.
> He so loved that He gave. It is the law of Christ Himself. He came
> through God's sacrifice and He came to sacrifice.[4]

The Father and the Son embraced sacrifice for the sake of the
lost. Their sacrifice enables lost children to be saved from darkness
and live in the light of Christ, sharing life with Him (see John 8:12).
We are the beneficiaries of the greatest sacrifice mankind has ever
known. The inheritance of God belongs to us through Jesus Christ
the Lord. Commenting on Christ's sacrifice, Simpson stated,

> [Christ] laid His honors down. . . . He made Himself one of them,
> and became a brother of this fallen race. . . . His whole life was a
> continual refusing of Himself, carrying their burdens and shar-
> ing their sorrows. And so love and sacrifice is the law of Christ.[5]

To Simpson, "the law of sacrifice [was] the greatest law in
earth and heaven."[6] The Master's life provided the only example
Simpson needed to follow in Christ's steps. In doing so he challenged others to join him in sacrificing for the cause of Christ.

However, it takes more than a challenge to motivate people to
embrace sacrifice. The authenticity, credibility and integrity of the
challenge is verified by a life that first sacrifices for Christ before
imploring others to do the same. A.B. Simpson lived such a life. His
spiritual journey is characterized by unending sacrifice in every
facet and dimension of his life. His ability to raise unprecedented
sums of money to advance the gospel of Christ at home and abroad
had little to do with his charismatic leadership. It had everything to
do with the Spirit's honoring the sacrifice of Christ's servant.

A.B. Simpson could stand before people with integrity of heart,
mind and life, challenging them to sacrifice for Christ's kingdom
because he was himself a man of sacrifice, qualified to call for self-
denying efforts to reach the neglected classes at their doors by work
adjusted to save them. This extended efforts abroad as well, answering the call to go into all the world and preach the gospel to all
men.[7] Simpson invited others to stand with him and be counted

among those who sacrificed so that unreached people could come to a personal saving relationship with Jesus Christ.

Sacrifice encompasses more than giving support to the ministries of those who serve at home and abroad. To Simpson, sacrifice meant giving yourself away in service to others. It involved the investment of your life into the lives of other people so they could experience the reality of Christ's love. Just as Christ gave Himself in service to others, so must we give ourselves in service to others for the sake of Christ. "The law of Christ is the bearing of others' burdens, the sharing of others' griefs, the sacrificing of yourself for others. [It] is the law of Christianity, the law of the saint."[8]

These are not words that Simpson merely preached from a pulpit or wrote in a magazine. They are a mirrored reflection of his life. He resigned a prestigious pastorate, relinquished all means of financial support, surrendered his credentials and left the denomination he had loved and served all of his life in order to devote himself to ministering to the huddled masses of immigrants streaming through New York City and the unreached people of foreign lands.

Simpson understood that sacrifice was something many Christians were unwilling to embrace. He notes that the great failure of the Christian life is the unwillingness to go with Christ all the way. Gethsemane and Calvary are places that demand or require more of ourselves than we want to give. To those who hesitate and waver, unwilling to present themselves as "living sacrifices," which is our "spiritual act of worship" (Romans 12:1), Simpson offers these words: "You have to go down into His death. . . . You have to go through it step by step. . . . It must be written on the records of your heart."[9]

PURE MOTIVES

It is in going with Christ all the way that we realize the fullest measure of satisfaction and joy in the Christ-life. It is in the discipline of sacrifice that we discover the secret to enlarging our faith. If the discovery is going to be made, the motive must be pure. Even the desire to grow in Christ can be tarnished by motives that are less than they should be. So Simpson cautions us to examine our motives and to realize that "our sacrifices and self-denials may be selfish. . . . We can have religious selfishness as well as carnal self-ishness."[10]

Simpson's words of caution flowed from the painful realization that good intentions threatened to tarnish his sacrifice. It was in confident expectation to the Lord's leading to launch a new ministry to the unreached masses of New York City that Simpson resigned his pastorate. With the resignation came the end of all means of financial support. Some would consider this the "first" step in a new work of faith. To Simpson, it was just "the next step" in a lifelong journey of faith. It was one of the endless number of steps of sacrifice that characterized his life and relationship with Jesus Christ. Simpson was confident that God would supply everything that was needed for this new work and meet all of his family's needs as well. How they would be supplied, he did not know.

With the passing of time financial matters concerning the support of his family began to take on a sense of urgency. Realizing that he was a gifted writer, Simpson concluded that he could support his family and possibly even the work through his literary talent. It seemed like a logical and reasonable thing to do. Shortly after this decision was made, Simpson sensed that it was being challenged. It was a challenge that he could not ignore or rationalize away. The Spirit had something to say to his heart and mind concerning the good-intentioned course of action he proposed to pursue.

Simpson stated, "[T]he Lord checked me from commercializing my gift."[11] God had other plans for supplying the needs. Christ's plans for Simpson's life and ministry were greater than anything he could have imagined. These plans required the undivided devotion of the servant to the pursuit of the work. Commercializing his ability to write would have clouded his focus, diluted his efforts and encumbered the advance of the gospel. It would have made his sacrifice less, far less, than an expression of wholehearted devotion to the Lord.

Finances were never the issue; the servant's undivided devotion and commitment to Christ were what mattered to God. Anything

Simpson could have made by writing for the commercial market would have been a mere pittance compared to the vast resources that would be needed to fund the work Christ was entrusting to him. A global missionary enterprise to the unreached peoples of the world requires resources only the Master can provide.

Simpson's words caution us about hidden dangers that may be associated with good intentions. Reasonable, logical conclusions that are in harmony with the good we are seeking to do in order to advance the work of Christ may threaten to tarnish the sacrifices we offer to the Lord. Admirable motives, godly ambition, kingdom priorities and a pure heart are not sufficient to guarantee the Lord's favor or acceptance of the sacrifices we are willing to make in the name of Jesus. We must also seek and know the mind of Christ. It is only then that we can be certain that the sacrifices we make and the way we make them are pure, pleasing and honoring to God.

THE ESSENTIAL SACRIFICE

Everything we posses is a gift from the Lord. God has entrusted all these things to us so that we may have the joy of using, even relinquishing, them in service to Christ. God wants us to delight in seeing the blessing other people experience as we pass on the trust that has been shared with us.

There are times when our serving Christ involves—even requires—sacrifice. The sacrifices Christians make in service to the cause of Christ are many and varied. They come in assorted shapes, sizes and forms. Some sacrifices are made without a moment's hesitation. Others involve difficulty and struggle as we anguish over releasing things that are precious to us. Suddenly, unexpectedly, we discover a battle raging deep within. With the mind we understand that we have to let go, but something in the heart is resisting. What makes it so difficult has nothing to do with selfishness. It has everything to do with something we did not expect. We never imagined that the Lord's blessing on our lives could have such a powerful hold upon our hearts. We never dreamed that a gift had the potential to become strong enough to rival, even challenge, our love and devotion to the Lord.

A strange, mysterious force is at work, exerting an influence upon our lives. The longer we hold on to it, the greater its hold upon our hearts becomes. Spiritual forces are at work. The Adversary is trying to seize an opportunity to hinder the fulfillment of Christ's purpose within and through our lives. Satan wants to make God's blessing a stumbling block that impedes the development of Christ's character in our lives.

A.B. Simpson recognized the nature of this spiritual battle. He knew the outward form could take on a variety of appearances suited to the Enemy's strategic advantage. He also understood the key to victory. To win, the essential sacrifice has to be made. The essential sacrifice is the pivotal point in our spiritual formation and development. Until this essential sacrifice is made, all of our sacrifices are merely steps leading to it. They are the outward evidence of the inward working of God's grace preparing for the decisive moment when we will make the essential sacrifice. Then, once it is made, every sacrifice we make flows from it. It is from this vantage point that we must view and understand sacrifice and the sacrifices Simpson made in his life and service to Jesus Christ.

Simpson summoned and challenged us to make this essential sacrifice, the sacrifice of ourselves unto God, in words challenging us to walk in the steps of Christ.

> The highest element of character is self-sacrifice, and here the Master stands forever in the front of all sacrifice. . . . Here we are taught what it means to walk even as He walked. It is the surrendered life. It is the life of self-sacrifice.[12]

Simpson was no stranger to the struggle involved in taking this step. He experienced it in his own life, and he knew the sense of apprehension that once filled his own heart could fill the hearts of others as well. To relieve their fears, he focused attention on God's loving care:

> We are not falling over a precipice or surrendering ourselves to the hands of a judge. Rather, we are sinking into a Father's arms and stepping into an infinite inheritance. It is an infinite privilege to be permitted thus to give ourselves up to One who pledges

Himself to make us all that we would love to be, all that His infinite wisdom, power and love will delight to accomplish in us.[13]

Simpson used every concept conveyed to the heart and mind by the thought of a Father who wants nothing but the very best for His child, to affirm and encourage us in taking this step with Christ. Love, acceptance, affirmation, contentment, fulfillment, peace, understanding, safety and security are just some of the concepts He used to encourage us to make the essential sacrifice, the sacrifice of ourselves to God.

He also hastened to add that this is not something that *we* are able to attain or accomplish.

> Sanctification is not your own work; it is not a gradual attainment which you can grow into by your own efforts. . . . You will grow after you are in sanctification into a fuller, riper and more mature development of life in Christ, but you must first take it at its commencement as a gift, not as a growth. It is an obtainment, not an attainment. You cannot sanctify yourself. The only thing to do is to give yourself wholly to God, a voluntary sacrifice. . . . He must do the work of cleansing and filling.[14]

This is a gift of God's redeeming grace. We are not promised the strength or goodness that is both needed and required to achieve this. It is achieved because God is at work within our hearts, "will[ing] and act[ing] according to his good purpose" (Philippians 2:13). So we are embracing the challenge to cooperate with the Father, Son and Spirit in bringing about that which God is seeking to accomplish within each believer's life. Simpson called it the sanctified life. It is a life that is set apart by the grace of God so that it may be completely dedicated to Him.

Taking the step to make this essential sacrifice means no holding back, no hanging on to something "just in case." It requires that we surrender all we have and all that we are to Jesus. Simpson declared:

> There must be, on our part, a complete surrender and self-renunciation, followed by a definite act of appropriating faith. . . . Through His gracious influence we present our bodies a living sacrifice, yield ourselves unto God in unreserved consecration, hand over to Him the old life of self and sin to be slain and buried forever, and

offer ourselves to His absolute ownership, possession, and disposition, unconditionally and irrevocably. The more definite and thorough this act of surrender, then the more complete and permanent will be the result. . . . He will accept a sincere and single desire, and will add His own perfect consecration to our imperfect act, thus making it acceptable to the Father through His grace.[15]

In taking this step, we surrender all that we know and all that we have to yield to God. We give to the Lord the innermost chamber of the heart, the fondest love and the things that are dearest and closest to us. It is when this sacrifice is made that Christ becomes our All-in-All. The spirit of self-sacrifice is the secret of true happiness.[16]

The motive, intention and desire of the heart are to voluntarily give the Lord all that there is to give. In the process of giving we find peace, joy, contentment and satisfaction that are greater than anything we have ever known.

Does this suggest that some issue will not be brought to light in the future? No, not at all. It means that if and when the Spirit, the searcher and revealer of our hearts, places something before us, this too will be offered up and given to the Lord. The essential sacrifice, the living sacrifice, is ongoing and continual. It never ceases.

Simpson's longing desire and prayer was that Christ would bring each of us to the point where we let go of life as a personal desire and give it to God as a living sacrifice. He also recognized that some who have walked with Christ for a period of time and who have gained a measure of spiritual development face a danger that has the power to keep them from taking the step that is needed to make the essential sacrifice. This danger involves the deception of the deadliest kind: self-deception. This is the danger the Apostle Paul identifies in challenging us to take the step and make the essential sacrifice. "Do not think of yourself more highly then you ought, but rather think of yourself with sober judgment, in accordance with the measure of faith God has given you" (Romans 12:3). Simpson understood the danger. He sought to caution and warn others in order to keep them from falling prey to this danger's snare.

There is no danger so great, especially among Christians somewhat advanced, as that of counting ourselves in a place where we really do not live. There is nothing so hardening to

the heart as to take the place of self-surrender and then live a
life of self-indulgence.[17]

Simpson reiterated his precautionary warning in *The Gospel of
Healing*. He reminded us that the life which has been touched by
God's grace must be lived for the honor and glory of Jesus Christ
and for the advancement of Christ's kingdom.

> Use your new strength and health for God, and be careful to obey
> the will of the Master. This Christ-given strength is a very sacred
> thing. It is the resurrection life of Christ in you. And it must be
> spent as He Himself would spend it. It cannot be wasted on sin
> and selfishness. It must be given to God as "a living sacrifice"
> (Romans 12:1).[18]

In summoning us to take this step, to make the essential sacrifice of offering ourselves to the Lord as a living sacrifice, Simpson
was inviting us to join him in presenting ourselves to God. The
cross is behind us. Life in Christ is before us. It is only as we surrender ourselves as living sacrifices that this life is lived and used
for Christ's service and glory.

An important decision in paving the way for Simpson to make
the essential sacrifice came when he was fourteen. Limited financial resources precluded the possibility of the family providing for-
mal education for any of the children except the oldest son. Young
Simpson understood and respected the decision. Yet he sensed the
call of God upon his life to pastoral ministry. Within his heart he
made the decision to make the sacrifices that were necessary to pay
the price. The only thing he asked for was his parents' permission
and blessing.

> I asked no money, no help, but only my father's blessing and
> consent, and I still remember the quiet, trembling tones with
> which he at last yielded and said, "God bless you, my boy, even if
> I cannot help you."
>
> So the struggle began, and I still never cease to thank God that
> it was a hard one. . . . Nothing under God was ever a greater
> blessing to me than the hard places which began with me nearly
> a half a century ago, and have never yet ceased.[19]

With his father's blessing, young Simpson proceeded to make the sacrifices necessary to prepare himself for the ministry. These steps of faith set into motion the final phase of the process which would culminate in Simpson's complete and total dedication to God three years later. The Apostle Paul's admonition, "I urge you, brothers, in view of God's mercy, to offer your bodies as living sacrifices, holy and pleasing to God—this is your spiritual act of worship" (Romans 12:1), became a reality in Simpson's life on January 19, 1861. That was the day that Albert Benjamin Simpson made the essential sacrifice of committing his life totally and completely to the Lord.

While reading Philip Doddridge's newly published book *The Rise and Progress of Religion in the Soul,* Simpson encountered a challenge to young Christians to write a statement declaring their devotion to Christ. The challenge could not be shaken or ignored. The Spirit was using Doddridge's words to speak to Simpson's heart. It was time to make a decision. It was a decision that required solitude, reflection, fasting and prayer. Simpson set aside a Saturday to be alone and draw close to God. It would be a day for the Spirit to examine the deep, innermost chambers of his heart and soul. The day concluded with Simpson's writing *A Solemn Covenant.* It was the written expression of his devotion and commitment to Jesus Christ as a living sacrifice.

Over the years some have suggested Simpson's covenant is too theologically developed to have been composed solely by the seventeen-year-old Simpson. Probably so. Some of the language and structure may have been borrowed from Doddridge, teachings and writings within Simpson's Reformed heritage and other sources. However, none of this changes one undeniable and crucial fact: Simpson's total commitment to Christ was expressed in *A Solemn Covenant.*

He made the essential sacrifice by offering his life as a living sacrifice to Christ. In the years to come Simpson would return to this moment. He would examine his life, his devotion and service to Christ, by the commitment he made that day. On September 1, 1863, and April 18, 1878, Simpson wrote comments on *A Solemn*

Covenant reaffirming the complete and unreserved commitment and dedication of his life to Jesus Christ.

A Sampling of Simpson's Sacrifices

By offering himself as a living sacrifice to God, A.B. Simpson was free to live his life as a sacrifice to Christ. Every facet and dimension of his life were an unending stewardship of the grace and riches of Jesus Christ. Samplings from three areas of Simpson's life illustrate the role sacrifice played in the ongoing development of his spiritual character.

These samplings are representative of his life with Christ. They include choosing the difficult path, the avenue of opportunity, that required more than he had to give. He correctly concluded that the difficult path would force him to rely upon the sufficiency of Christ. Financial sacrifice and loss comprise the second sampling. We will discover that Simpson chose financial sacrifice so every available resource could be channeled into fulfilling the work of Christ. Finally, Simpson sacrificed his reputation and name to pursue the vision Christ placed within his soul. This sampling does not exhaust the illustrations that could be cited to show the role the discipline of sacrifice played in the formation and continuation of his life and ministry. They merely provide a window to view his soul.

As a newly accredited candidate for pastoral ministry, Simpson made a decision that would typify his approach to ministry throughout the years. He was faced with a choice. He could accept a call to serve a congregation he could easily care for, or he could assume a pastorate with many demanding and time-consuming responsibilities. As he stated it, Simpson was faced with a choice between

> . . . two fields of labor; one an extremely easy one, in a delightful town, with a refined, affectionate, and prosperous church, just large enough to be an ideal field for one who wished to spend a few years in quiet preparation for future usefulness; the other, a large, absorbing city church, with many hundreds of members

and overwhelming and heavy burdens, which were sure to demand the utmost care, labor and responsibility. All my friends,
teachers and counsellors advised me to take the easier place.[20]

He considered their counsel, but he decided to accept the call to
the field that would demand and require more. Simpson explained
his decision by saying,

If I take the small church it will demand little, and I will give little. Result, stagnation; I will get soft and cease to grow. If I take
the large church I will be compelled to rise to meet its heavier demands, and the very effort will develop the gifts of God which
are in me. The small church may break me; the large church will
certainly help to make me.[21]

Simpson chose the difficult place. Knox Church in Hamilton,
Ontario, had been floundering without pastoral leadership for
nearly eighteen months. The declining congregation hoped the arrival of a young pastor would help revitalize the church. Their hopes
were not disappointed. The years of service in Hamilton not only re-
vitalized the church, but they were also instrumental in shaping
and refining the personal habits and disciplines Simpson needed to
seize the opportunities Christ would soon place before him. Reflecting on this pastorate, Simpson said, "My early ministry was developed, and the habit of venturing on difficult undertakings was
largely established, by the grace of God, through the necessities of
this difficult position."[22]

The experiences in Hamilton caused Simpson to rely upon the
grace and sufficiency of God. The objective Simpson sought to
achieve by serving in the harder place was accomplished. The experience solidified the way he would approach ministry throughout
his life. Simpson would encourage us to choose the difficult path, to
select the opportunity that demands more than we have to give, to
welcome the service that requires nothing less than our complete
reliance upon the sufficiency of Christ.

This is the objective the discipline of sacrifice seeks to accomplish. In every city in which Simpson served, the passion burning
in his soul fueled the vision for a greater work. He never understood "greater" in terms of prominence or prestige. These were

foreign concepts to Simpson's way of thinking. These things had nothing to do with greatness. In Simpson's eyes a greater work was a work propelled by sacrifice to penetrate the darkness with the message and presence of Christ. "Greater" was understood in terms of people, unreached people, touched by the love, grace and transforming power of the gospel of salvation.

Each sacrifice proved the faithfulness of God and paved the way for the sacrifices that would be required to achieve even more for Jesus. The vision of unreached people stirring within his soul would set the stage for Simpson to make even greater sacrifices to advance the gospel.

The opportunity to serve in New York City thrust the Simpson household into uncharted waters that would test their love for each other and their devotion to Christ. Mrs. Simpson recoiled at the thought of relocating to New York City. She could not imagine raising a family in that environment.

Simpson viewed the possibility of serving in New York City as God's answer to the passion burning within his soul. The thousands upon thousands of people streaming into America represented the unreached masses from the regions beyond. He wanted to be where they were. This was an opportunity to share the hope, love and message of Christ with those coming to America seeking to start a new life.

Simpson knew that New York City was more than the entry point to America: It was the gateway to the world. The urban setting provided a cosmopolitan environment that fostered a global mind-set. People were accustomed to thinking internationally. This was the ideal place to share his missionary vision. It was here that he would find the fertile soil to nurture the vision so it could blossom and grow. Simpson's decision to accept the call to serve in New York City was forged by a vision for the unreached people of the world.

Within his heart and mind Simpson was convinced that he was saying yes to the Lord's leading even though he knew his wife was not sympathetic to the move. The intervening months were marked by marital stress and tension within the home. Entries in Simpson's diary reveal the conflict that took place.

> She is possessed of an intense bitterness, and I am full of pain
> and fear. . . . Great trials today about Margaret. . . . My wife is in a
> state of hardness and rebellion. Lord, help me to feel, act and
> pray aright. . . . Alternate feelings of compassion, tenderness and
> dreadful pain and even fear about Maggie, who is so set in her
> seeming hatred to me that I can hardly speak to her. I have shut
> myself up in my Savior, leaving her simply and fully with Him.[23]

Simpson's diary entries never frame the conflict in terms of something a husband or a wife could have done differently. His vision penetrated beneath the surface and beyond the obvious. He viewed it solely in terms of a spiritual struggle that he sought to resolve by relying on the sufficiency of God.

It was a conflict that would take time to diffuse. There were things the Spirit needed to accomplish in both of their lives. The Lord would have to enlarge the vision of Margaret Simpson's heart so she could see and embrace the global trust Christ was committing to her husband. Such a vast field of service was far beyond anything she ever imagined possible when she became a pastor's wife.

There were things A.B. Simpson had to learn as well. If people were going to share his vision for taking the gospel to the unreached people of the world, he would have to learn to wait upon the Lord. He would have to linger long enough for the vision to fill their hearts and for the burden to flood their souls. Once it seized them, nothing would hold them back. This was a journey that Albert and Margaret Simpson needed to make together. For that to happen, Christ would have to do something in both of them.

A sampling of the entries found in Simpson's diary during this difficult period reveal the longing of his soul.

> Lord, help me to feel, act and pray aright. . . . I trust my own heart
> may be kept righteous, and merciful in everything. . . . Help me to
> leave all these cares upon Thee—be independent of all natural
> feelings and filled with God. . . . I thank God for the wonderful
> discipline through which He has led my soul, the suffering and
> power that has come out of it. I pray for grace to walk in the
> Spirit wholly, always yielded to His will, trusting perfectly, tri-
> umphing over all sin and doubt and pleasing my Father blame-
> lessly. For a Christian temper and attitude toward my wife in

everything, so as fully to please God and never regret a word, act or thought.[24]

Simpson was as concerned for the enlargement of his own heart as he was for his wife's. God's grace proved sufficient. In God's time, changes took place in both of their hearts. Concerning his wife Simpson wrote, "Praise for my wife's kind and loving and altered spirit. God seems to bless her as He leads me in the path He has clearly shown."[25]

Accepting the call to serve a New York City pastorate marked the beginning of financial sacrifice for the Simpsons. The rest of their lives would be characterized by financial sacrifice for the sake of advancing the cause of Christ. The move to New York City involved a significantly lower salary and a considerably higher cost of living.[26] The financial repercussions of the move undoubtedly contributed to the strain in their marriage.

Shortly after their relocation to New York City, Simpson's diary records a comment expressing delight at the money he was able to save by making a bookcase instead of buying one.[27] This suggests something about the financial strain the Simpson household was seeking to cope with. One could only imagine the tension involved in trying to make do.

It was a tension that certainly escalated when Simpson spent the $555 Christmas gift he received from the church on publishing costs associated with the new missionary magazine he was attempting to publish. He viewed the gift as God's unexpected supply to meet the needs of this new publishing venture to promote missions. It is likely that Mrs. Simpson saw it instead as God's way of providing for the family's growing financial needs.

In less than two years A.B. Simpson would make a crucial decision that underscored his determination to sacrifice everything to advance the work of Christ. Seeing and meeting the immigrants coming to America fanned the flames of the passion within his soul. Their response to his ministry fueled his vision for taking the message of salvation to the unreached people of the world. The confines of pastoral ministry could not begin to contain the desire of his heart.

Convinced that the Lord was leading him into a global ministry, Simpson submitted his pastoral resignation from Thirteenth Street Presbyterian Church on November 7, 1881. Committed to the sufficiency of God's grace, with no following, organization or financial resources, but with a family to support, and with his most intimate ministerial friends and associates predicting failure, Simpson walked away with nothing but a vision burning in his soul to begin a new work.

The coming weeks, months and years would prove Simpson's unwavering determination to sacrifice in order to advance the message of Christ. They would also bear testimony to the faithfulness and the sufficiency of God. He never considered finances or material things as something to possess. They were merely tools to use in propagating the gospel. His stewardship of God's grace demanded that he use them well.

Those who shared a vision for the lost of other nations were attracted to Simpson's visionary leadership. The Gospel Tabernacle was founded as a place for worship and as a base for training and equipping believers to share their faith at home and abroad. "Every cent that came into his coffers by way of contributions went to support the work of the Society."[28] In all the years that Simpson served this thriving congregation, he never accepted a salary. As the founder and president of The Christian and Missionary Alliance, he never received the living allowance granted missionaries and executive officers of the Society. He frequently refused to accept traveling expenses to missionary conventions.[29]

The financial sacrifices Simpson had made in the past prepared him for a life of sacrifice. He would spend everything he received to take the message of Christ's redeeming love to the unreached huddled masses of the world. A.W. Tozer observed,

> Not until his old age did he receive one cent from his spiritual labors, and then only because the men of his board issued a good-natured ultimatum and compelled him to agree to receive a small allowance for his last days."[30]

In the twilight years of his life, some of Simpson's close friends chipped in and paid off his outstanding indebtedness. He had nothing of any value to leave his family.[31]

There is one area of sacrifice Simpson experienced that must not be overlooked. News of his pastoral resignation to launch a new work would mean the sacrifice of his reputation and name. These were placed on the altar as Simpson followed the heavenly vision to begin a new work for Jesus Christ. The scorn came through the hands of fellow ministers. Kenneth Mackenzie writes,

> Satire, censure and condemnation were freely offered him. Editors of church papers hurled their javelins; contributors to the magazines dipped their pens in gall; preachers denounced the fallacy in terms of unstinted severity. He gladly drank the bitter cup, persuaded that he was in the will of God.[32]

The undeniable evidence of God's favor upon this new movement did not stop critical tongues from lashing out at Simpson. Instead of affirming him, they belittled his vision and tried to thwart his success. Perhaps it was a spirit of envy or jealousy that caused them to oppose him. Did they foolishly think they could stem the tide of God's blessing?

> As [the missionary conventions] grew in importance they quite naturally drew the fire of that large section of the Christian public which was opposed to all the doctrines and practices for which Mr. Simpson stood.[33]

Instead of joining hands and partnering together with Simpson, they tried to block his efforts. Attacks were launched against his approach to ministry. Simpson knew that lost people were not going to walk into a Sunday worship service looking for salvation. He observed that Christians were not as diligent or aggressive in seeking to reach the lost in their communities as they could be. So Simpson sought to take the message to the people. Realizing that the most popular meeting place in the community was the theater, Simpson rented the places the people frequented and met them there.

The response was phenomenal. People came and they did not stop coming. Night after night overflowing crowds of unreached people filled the theater and encountered the love, hope, forgiveness and peace of Jesus Christ. When it was no longer possible to ignore the success of Simpson's efforts, critics voiced their opposition to Simpson and his methods. Their words were couched in terms that seemed to express a concern for the purity of the gospel by saying, "It cheapens the Gospel to take it to a theatre; it lowers the prestige of the Christian religion to go to a place of worldly amusement to pray."[34]

Perhaps they were too insecure or territory-conscious to realize that by working together they could accomplish more for Christ than any of them could ever hope to accomplish on their own. Maybe they were speaking against Simpson because they were not mobilizing their own congregations to reach people for Jesus Christ.

Even those who once cooperated in supporting Simpson's efforts began pulling away. The success of his missionary endeavor grew to such proportions that some decided to redirect the focus of their resources to their own ministries. Instead of partnering with Simpson, they would recruit, train and send their own missionaries. Kenneth Mackenzie, rector of Holy Trinity Church in Westport, Connecticut, lecturer at the Nyack Missionary Training Institute and friend of Simpson writes, "No missionary board would take his candidates; no church would pay their way."[35] Undaunted by these developments, Simpson forged ahead. The work continued to grow and develop.

Still there were some in the Christian community lingering in the shadows. They were waiting for the opportune time to take one last parting shot at A.B. Simpson. The shot came while the members of the Alliance family and friends grieved the loss of their visionary leader, missionary statesman and friend. As the baton of leadership was being passed to those who would carry on the work, one final volley sought to discredit the life and ministry of this man who lived to serve God. An eminent official of one prominent mission board said, "The Missionary Alliance would have to crumble; for it had no head to direct it, no foundation upon which to build."[36]

The critics were wrong. The work did not wither and die. It continues to flourish and grow. Thousands upon thousands of people from the nations of the world make up the Alliance today. They are the beneficiaries who share the spiritual heritage and inheritance of this man, a man of faith and sacrifice for Jesus Christ.

Simpson's life exemplified a life of sacrifice. It was a life given back to God because of the sacrifice of Jesus Christ. Every time Simpson let go of something to follow Jesus, the Lord honored him by giving him "true riches." Sacrifice was more than a spiritual discipline for Simpson: It was his way of life. He embraced it so others could possess all the spiritual riches of eternal life through Jesus Christ.

George Sandison, editor of *The Christian Herald*, wrote, "I can think of no one in this age who has done more effective, self-denying service for Christ and His Gospel than Albert B. Simpson."[37] Albert Benjamin Simpson considered "everything a loss compared to the surpassing greatness of knowing Christ Jesus [his] Lord, for whose sake [he had] lost all things . . . that [he might] gain Christ" (Philippians 3:8).

The inevitable question looming before us is obvious. Are we willing to follow Simpson's steps and embrace a life and discipline of sacrifice that others may come to know the redeeming love of Jesus Christ? Are we willing to take the difficult path, or are we content to settle for opportunities that require little? Are we willing to embrace financial sacrifice for the sake of the cause of Christ? Will we follow in the steps that advance the cause of Christ even though others speak against our name?

CONSIDERATIONS FOR YOUR SPIRITUAL DEVELOPMENT

Sacrifice is a not a familiar concept to many people. They may have heard of it but have no idea what it means to voluntarily embrace it.

People who call attention to what they have given up or are doing without for someone else's benefit are not making a sacrifice. They are either playing the role of a martyr, trying to make a name for themselves, or they are letting others know that they "owe them." Those who embrace the discipline of sacrifice don't call attention to themselves or what they are doing. Their sacrifices are expressions of their love for the Lord and the people the Lord loves. Expressing this love is all that really matters to them.

● ● ● ● ● ● ● ● ● ● ● ● ● *Application*

1. Can you recall a time when you realized that someone made a sacrifice that benefitted you?

2. Describe the emotions you experienced when you discovered that you were the beneficiary of someone's sacrifice, service, love and grace.

3. Explain how the sacrifice you make today is a down payment that positions you to make the next sacrifice necessary to continue growing. How has this principle been true in your life?

4. Pause and reflect on the sacrifice Jesus Christ made for you. Note some of the benefits and blessings that are available to you because of His sacrifice.

5. Since you are the beneficiary of God's grace, have you considered making any sacrifices so that others may know Jesus? List the types of sacrifices you could make for the cause of Christ out of your love for Jesus (e.g., time given to intercessory prayer, service, meeting needs; financial gifts or offerings in service to Christ; etc.).

6. Now that you have an idea of the types of sacrifices you could make, what do you sense God would have you do? If you are not sure, that is OK! Make this a matter of prayer and listen for the Lord's voice to confirm what Jesus would have you do. Equally important is sensing God's timing for doing it. Some of the most effective sacrifices are the simplest. The gift of time in ministering to others can be a powerful tool in the hand of God that touches the hearts and souls of others with the convincing proof of God's love and grace. Remember: Everything we possess is a gift from the Lord. Blessed are those who let God's blessing pass through their hands to another in the name of Jesus.

Chapter FIVE

LETTING GO OF THINGS THAT SLOW YOU DOWN
Living with *Simplicity*

Simplicity was the complementary companion that accompanied A.B. Simpson's life of sacrifice. He witnessed the place simplicity had in his parents' lives. They exemplified the virtue of simplicity, the value of contentment and the role simplicity can play in furthering the cause of Christ.

Simplicity flows from the heart to the outward behaviors of life. Sensing God's call to prepare for ministry, coupled with the realization that his parents did not have the resources to help him with college, Simpson embraced this discipline.

Simplicity is an avenue that allows us to draw close to God and to reach out in service to others in Jesus' name. It liberates us from the world's enticements. We are not compelled to listen to the endless stream of voices summoning us to the things the world values. We are free to live in single-minded unity and devotion to God. In *Disciplines of the Holy Spirit,* Tan and Gregg observe:

> The Spirit works through the spiritual discipline of simplicity to keep our focus on God and His kingdom, helping us to reach out to others. As He leads us into simplicity, He will bring our character and lifestyle into a simple-minded obedience to God's will and conformity to the image of Christ.[1]

A SHARPENED FOCUS

A life of simplicity is a natural consequence of a life presented to Christ as a living sacrifice. Sacrifice and simplicity go together.

Simplicity enables Christ's followers to maximize the potential of their resources and the sacrifices they gladly make in service to Christ. "The central point for the discipline of simplicity is to seek the kingdom of God and the righteousness of his kingdom first, and then everything necessary will come in its proper place."[2]

A.B. Simpson witnessed the conflict that developed within the Canadian Presbyterian church as proponents of simplicity clashed with those advocating the construction of more elaborate facilities. Architectural design became a controversial battlefield for Canadian Presbyterians. In the Reformed tradition of the day, places of worship were rather simple or plainly constructed buildings, reflecting the austere Reformed emphasis upon the Scriptures. As the people prospered, congregations started to build larger, more elaborate, imposing edifices. This soon become the norm for many urban Presbyterians.[3]

Church architecture was an issue that erupted into an irreconcilable conflict in Simpson's Louisville, Kentucky, pastorate. The session overwhelmingly endorsed Simpson's proposal to relocate and build a new facility in the midst of the city's greatest concentration of unchurched people. A new facility strategically located and accessible to the city's unreached population, in addition to an aggressive outreach ministry, would win many to Christ.

The plan called for a spacious but economically constructed tabernacle. Simplicity in structure and design were crucial: The unreached masses had to perceive the building as a place where they would be welcome and feel comfortable. An elaborate facility would pose a hindrance to the evangelistic objectives the church was seeking to achieve. Simpson also knew the possessive tendency of the human heart. The congregation could develop a territorial attitude that resented newcomers who were unable to help meet the church's financial obligations. The mere detection of such an attitude would thwart their evangelistic objective and alienate them from the very people they were seeking to bring into Christ's kingdom.

In addition to these concerns, Simpson did not want to incur indebtedness. He wanted to avoid the costly entanglements involved in servicing a debt. The prospect of mortgaging their future and tying up the congregation's resources for years was not acceptable to him. He felt that instead of ministering to others, the congregation's energies would be spent trying to free themselves from financial bondage.

Simpson wanted the freedom to channel the resources Jesus entrusted to the congregation into new ministry initiatives that would convey the reality of Christ's love and declare the hope of salvation. He knew that if the congregation failed to embrace simplicity, this failure would hinder the objectives they were hoping to accomplish by taking this step of faith. The opportunity for blessing, salvation and the joyful realization that Christ was using them to expand the kingdom of God could be lost.

The trustees did not share Simpson's commitment to simplicity. If they were going to build a new facility, it was going to have all the amenities the people wanted. The spirit of and commitment to simplicity residing within Simpson's heart was not shared by the congregation. His pleas for simplicity fell upon deaf ears. Plans were changed, construction costs multiplied, and indebtedness soared. Building costs exceeded the original estimate by seventy percent. They had succeeded in constructing a magnificent architectural edifice, but in the process of doing so, they had failed to achieve their objective. The building was too ornate, too elaborate, to convey a sense of welcome to the people they originally intended to reach. They could not afford to initiate new ministries.

The day for dedicating a new church should be a time of joyous celebration. The congregation is supposed to give thanks and rejoice over the prospects of an expanded and enlarged ministry to their city. Instead it was a time of heaviness and pleading. In Simpson's mind the building did not belong to the Lord, and would not until the people were willing to make the sacrifice to make it free and clear of debt. He sensed the moment of opportunity slipping away. Yet maybe it could be salvaged. He was convinced that a bold sacrificial effort by the people could completely eliminate the indebtedness, freeing them from financial bondage and releasing them into new opportunities for Christ's kingdom. He stood before the congregation and made one final appeal:

> It will expose us to just criticism if we have built a home we cannot afford to own. It will prove a fetter to our freedom and our energies. Church debts are properly called *church bonds*.

There are two things this church must be if it is to be blessed. One is, *it must be free*, free in the full sense that all shall give gladly, freely to God according to their means. . . . The other is *it must be unselfish and missionary*. If this Tabernacle is not able to give up every year as much to the great cause of the conversion of the world as to its own support, it stands as a living embodiment of selfishness and will die of chills. Now a church with bonds cannot be a successful missionary church. Every call for the conversion of the world will be answered by the low, sullen word—debt. . . . And therefore the easiest way would be to make one brave, final sacrifice. . . . This morning I desire to place on this pulpit the simple standard, *Broadway Tabernacle Free!* free from debt, free to God, free to all.[4]

This was not to be. Those who could have responded refused. The plans to dedicate the new building were set. They were going ahead with the dedication service with or without their pastor's approval. He was the one who challenged them to take this step of faith, so how could he say no to the vision birthed within his own soul?

Perhaps they failed to comprehend the importance and the value of simplicity in the life and the ministry of their pastor. Maybe they did not understand that the building was never intended to be anything more than a means to an end—an end of bringing lost people to Christ the Lord.

Deep within his own heart, A.B. Simpson could not bring himself to dedicate a building to the glory of God that was burdened by debt. The service concluded without a dedication.

The objective of simplicity is to help God's children reach out in love and service to others in the name of Christ. With a broken heart Simpson saw his congregation lose that objective by refusing to display the strength and courage needed to embrace the discipline of simplicity.

DEPENDENCE ON CHRIST'S SUFFICIENCY

Certainly the bitter pain of this experience lingered in Simpson's being a long time. However, it did not deter him from pursuing simplicity. He wanted to be free, free to employ every available resource to advance the kingdom of God. He was determined to avoid indebtedness and to live free from dependence upon things. The only dependence he desired was complete and total dependence upon the sufficiency of Jesus Christ.

In a matter of a few brief years the Spirit would lead Simpson into an entirely new role of ministry in New York City. He resigned from the pastoral ministry to launch a new work to the unreached masses at home and abroad. One of the early steps in this new venture with Christ was establishing a nucleus of people who shared the vision for reaching the unreached people of the world. As the core group grew larger, the need for a place for them to meet had to be addressed.

Shifting the location of meetings from place to place was not conducive to the growth of the movement. Following several months of prayer for this need, Simpson paused to remind the people what they were praying for and what the answer to their prayers would look like.

> It only remained to be added that for many months the hearts of
> the people have been led to pray for a permanent home for this
> work in the form of a simple Gospel Tabernacle, built in the most
> economical way and capable of seating the largest number of
> people possible.[5]

Once again we see Simpson consciously underscoring his commitment to simplicity, coupled with its connection of furthering the work of Christ. These were inherently related in Simpson's thoughts. There was no way to separate them.

As the movement continued to grow, Simpson formed the missionary society known as The Christian and Missionary Alliance. His commitment to simplicity played a primary role in establishing the fiscal policies of the Alliance. In the president's address to the Annual Council of the Alliance in March 1914, Simpson stated, "This is an economical movement avoiding expensive establishments, aiming to make every dollar go as far as possible, and sending only such missionaries who are glad to give their lives and services for their bare expenses."[6]

Extravagance had no place in Simpson's way of thinking. Neither did needless indulgence or luxury. Necessities were defined as the bare essentials needed to continue advancing the work. Responsible stewardship meant the wise and prudent expenditure of the resources Christ had entrusted to His people.

Robert Ekvall explained another reasoning behind the simplicity that characterized Simpson's leadership:

> Money that came from earnest people who gave sacrificially out of . . . humble circumstances was earmarked by that sacrifice for only the most economical use. No large salaries could be paid, no premiums for skill, ability, and experience could be given. Thus, the pro rate distribution of what in their maximum were only intended to be living allowances, became the basic principle of financial demonstration.[7]

A.B. Simpson never lost sight of the sacrifice involved in the gifts and offerings that were given to further the cause of Christ by the people supporting The Christian and Missionary Alliance. He knew that standing behind the financial contributions were countless numbers of men and women embracing the discipline of simplicity so they could make even greater sacrifices for the sake of the call. Any financial policy that failed to respect and honor the sacrifice of the people was a policy that was not worthy of Christ or the Church.

Simpson's statements underscore the fundamental principles that determined the level of compensation that would be provided for those who went into service for the Lord. The salaries and allowances the workers received were minimal. Financial incentives were nonexistent. The idea of offering comparable compensation to attract the best and most qualified was unheard of. Notions such as these were contrary to the principles of simplicity and sacrifice.

Some may wonder how Simpson managed to recruit people to serve. How was he continually able to amass a missionary force, the educators and support personnel to sustain, let alone advance, this missionary movement in new areas? The answer to this and similar questions is simple: The attraction and dedication to the cause had nothing to do with the level of financial remuneration.

The answer is found in three vital forces. First is the vision. Simpson attracted people because of his commitment to the vision and Christ's call. There was not the slightest reservation in his heart or mind concerning what Christ had called him to do. He shared the vision with people and they committed themselves to that vision. They wanted to be a part of something the Spirit was accomplishing throughout the world. They wanted to share in a vision that could only be accomplished through the sufficiency of God and the empowering of the Holy Spirit.

Second, God honored Christ's servant. A.B. Simpson never asked or expected of others something that he was not already committed to or doing. This kind of determination produces a Spirit-known and -confirmed integrity that imparts an authenticating credibility that cannot be denied. It draws people who want to stand, partner and work with those who are already demonstrating the devotion and commitment to the Lord that involves discipline and sacrifice.

Third, there was Simpson's commitment to the success of the people who served with him. It was not his ministry; it was theirs. It was not his success; it was theirs. Every advance, every victory was theirs. When missionaries left for the field, Simpson was there to see them off. When they returned, he was there to greet them. While they were gone, he was on his knees interceding and praying for them. Their work was something he shared with the people as he sought to raise prayer and financial support for them. Simpson was not only their leader, but he was their intercessor, advocate and friend.

Simpson never put himself above them. He served Christ beside them. His determination to do this was demonstrated in his response to those who awarded and conferred on him an honorary doctor of divinity degree. The degree was bestowed in recognition of Simpson's scholastic achievements, worldwide leadership and sterling character.

> After due thought, and no doubt much prayer, he returned the parchment and the doctor's hood, with an appreciative expression of his recognition and [their] kindness. But in his letter he made clear that in doing so, he would have the faculty and trustees realize his only plea, that the restraint he felt in being in any measure exalted above the lowliest of his brethren; and as well,

lest in accepting this distinction, he might fail of the Lord's benediction and his work lose the divine approval.[8]

A.B. Simpson wanted to stand beside those who served in the
cause of Christ. The mere perception of being above them was not
acceptable to him. He understood that it is because of the grace of
Jesus Christ that any of us have the privilege of accomplishing
anything that matters. The Apostle Paul's words were written in
the fiber of Simpson's soul.

> What, after all, is Apollos? And what is Paul? Only servants,
> through whom you came to believe—as the Lord has assigned to
> each his task. I planted the seed, Apollos watered it, but God made
> it grow. So neither he who plants nor he who waters is anything,
> but only God, who makes things grow. (1 Corinthians 3:5-7)

Simpson never lost sight of one undeniable and fundamental
understanding: The increase comes from the Lord. The call, the
abilities, the spiritual gifts, the empowering and the results are
all the work of God.

APPRECIATION OF TRUE WORTH

This is the beauty of the discipline of simplicity. The cultural
rewards, honors and accolades society bestows do not define or
determine our worth in the sight of Jesus Christ. By God's grace
we are partners laboring together in the field according to the
measure of the grace given to us by the Lord Jesus Christ.

It was for the glory of Jesus Christ that A.B. Simpson pursued
simplicity in his personal life, in his pastoral ministry and as the visionary founder of the new missionary society known as The Christian and Missionary Alliance. Today evangelicals have entered a
new millennium. The burning passion of Simpson's soul for the
salvation of those living in the regions beyond the presence and influence of the gospel of Jesus Christ fuels our hope for the future.
Unprecedented opportunities for advancing the gospel and winning the lost are before us on virtually every continent.

Taking advantage of these opportunities requires substantial increases in giving. Funding the vision involves sacrifice. It always
does. It also means that we must be wise, faithful stewards of the

resources committed to us. Following in Simpson's steps is not an option; it is nothing less than an absolute necessity. We must demonstrate this godly man's commitment to simplicity. This is a commitment that runs contrary to our culture.

We live in an era of indulgence. This in and of itself provides a stunning background for people to view simplicity. Increasing numbers of people in our society are turning from our culture's dictates and embracing lifestyles of simplicity. They are discovering the contentment that comes with less. If this is perceived as beneficial within the secular realm, how much more worth and value does it have in the spiritual realm? How much more could God's children accomplish in compassionate service for Christ by choosing to live more simply? Perhaps far more than we will ever imagine.

An observation was made concerning A.B. Simpson that caused people to live more simply and to follow him in sacrificing for the advance of Christ's kingdom. W.R. Moody, editor of *Record of Christian Work*, wrote,

> The thing that impresses me more than anything else in Dr. Simpson was the faithfulness of his Christian stewardship. . . . Realizing that he had the ear of the Christian public, he looked upon this as that for which he should give a strict account of his stewardship.[9]

This observation inspired people to support the cause in order to advance the work. They knew that personal advantage and material gain were never an issue to Simpson. Everything in his life was subservient to the ministry of the gospel of Christ. Simpson wanted to be found faithful in using the resources God placed in his care to advance the Lord's kingdom.

The vital link between simplicity, advancing the gospel and meeting the material needs of others was something Simpson clearly understood. Touching lives at the point of their material needs, alleviating the misery and pain of human suffering, confirms the compassion of Christ. It affirms the dignity of our fellowman while underscoring the individual's worth as a human being. In many cases it opens the doors to hearts and provides us with the opportunity to share the message of Christ.

A lack of response or interest in spiritual things should not deter or hinder us from demonstrating the compassion of Christ. Knowing that this is what Jesus did, regardless of the response, is all the reason we need to follow in Christ's steps. We are not trying to do this to impress other people or to feel good about ourselves. We are doing it because we are committed to emulating the life of Christ.

We are stewards of the resources God has placed in our care. Living more simply enhances our prospects of touching human souls with the compassionate love of Jesus Christ. Resources are freed from other things in order to advance Christ's gospel. This is something the Apostle Peter's words impressed upon Simpson's heart.

> The day of the Lord will come like a thief. The heavens will disappear with a roar; the elements will be destroyed by fire, and the earth and everything in it will be laid bare. Since everything will be destroyed in this way, what kind of people ought you to be? You ought to live holy and godly lives as you look forward to the day of God and speed its coming. (2 Peter 3:10-12)

A.B. Simpson embraced simplicity as a discipline that caused him to draw closer to God. This alone should be a compelling and sufficient reason for us to embrace this spiritual discipline in our own lives and walk with Christ. However, the significance of simplicity is even greater than our personal edification.

Simplicity is effective in furthering the spread of the gospel to the unreached people of the world. It maximizes the use of our resources and multiplies the benefits that can be achieved for the glory of Christ. Embracing this discipline calls for the courage and conviction to make difficult choices. Personal preferences and pet projects must be recognized for what they are—things that have the potential to impede the work of Christ.

Simplicity is more than a spiritual discipline that characterized A.B. Simpson's life and ministry. Simplicity is an indispensable tool in our arsenal for accomplishing Christ's mission of reaching the lost with the gospel of salvation and developing men and women in the maturity and fullness of Christ. It is a vital resource for advancing Christ's kingdom and drawing us even closer to God in the process.

CONSIDERATIONS FOR YOUR SPIRITUAL DEVELOPMENT

The time in which we live thrives on personal indulgence. Our senses are constantly bombarded with advertisements and publicity enticing us to spend what we don't have to purchase what we don't need. People across our nation are staggering under a burden that pushes them to the point of despair. Their lives are so cluttered with stuff and juggling financial responsibilities that they do not have the time or the energy to focus on maintaining, let alone developing, their relationships with God or sharing their faith with others.

Embracing the discipline of simplicity has the potential to free us from the power of things that complicate and consume our lives. I use the word *potential,* because the moment we begin trying to live without these things is the moment we discover the power hold they have on every part of our lives. Those who are unwilling to let go will never enter into the freedom simplicity offers.

● ● ● ● ● ● ● ● ● ● ● ● *Application*

1. Take time to consider how our society seeks to foster a spirit of discontentment with what we have. Make note of some of the things advertisers do to convince us that what they are selling is something we "must" have.
2. Walk through your basement, garage, storage shed or attic and take a brief inventory of the "must-have" things that you didn't need. (This could be discouraging!) Ask yourself, did these things really make a difference in your life? Since it is impossible to turn back the hands of time, determine to make these must-have things a reminder of what you don't really need.

3. Pray and ask the Lord to teach you to appreciate and to be content with what you have.
4. Seek the Lord's direction for ways to live more simply.
5. Talk to people who practice the discipline of simplicity. Listen to their stories and discover how simplicity released them from the tyranny of things. Discover how simplicity benefits their lives with Christ and furthers their own spiritual development.
6. Think of the good you could do for the cause of Christ if you lived more simply. What are you going to do about it?

Chapter SIX

ENJOYING GOD'S PRESENCE
The Blessing of *Solitude*

The disciplines of solitude and silence have complementary roles in spiritual formation and development. Solitude and silence are crucial components of each other. In fact, they are so much a part of each other that they are nearly inseparable. There may be occasions when there is silence without solitude, but there will never be a time when there is solitude without silence. Together, the disciplines of solitude and silence played a crucial, ongoing role in the formation and development of A.B. Simpson's spiritual character and maturity.

Solitude unfolds in two dimensions. First, there is solitude that is in response to Jesus' invitation: "Come with me by yourselves to a quiet place and get some rest" (Mark 6:31). Christ's disciples were invited to join Jesus in doing something they had seen Him do in the past and would certainly see Him do again in the future. It is an invitation to step away from people and the expectations and demands of life and ministry to be alone and draw close to God.

This drawing close to God is what distinguishes solitude from isolation. There is a purpose in getting away. That purpose is to seek the Father and draw close to the presence of the Almighty. Jesus' example and invitation summon us to follow in the steps of a spiritual discipline that is an essential part of life in Christ.

There is another dimension of solitude that is not of our own choosing. It is the solitude the Spirit forces, imposes—even thrusts—upon us so God may accomplish something deep within our souls. It is in this moment of divine choosing, usually involving circumstances and events we would never think of embracing, that the Spirit brings about a transformation of our inner beings. Through this often painful process we emerge more like Jesus and closer to God than we have ever been before. St. John of the Cross called this time of solitude "the dark night of the soul."

This dimension of solitude was known to A.W. Tozer. In his formative years Tozer was strongly influenced by A.B. Simpson. Tozer went on to become an Alliance pastor, spokesman, author and editor of the denominational periodical *The Alliance Weekly*. In his book *That Incredible Christian*, Tozer refers to this kind of solitude as "the ministry of the night."[1] It is a ministry the Spirit used at pivotal points and crucial junctures in Simpson's life to shape, refine, confirm and prove his spiritual character, ministry and vision.

Simpson emerged from "the ministry of the night" stronger, closer and more devoted to Christ than ever before. There was a connection between this outcome and Simpson's determination to embrace the discipline of solitude early in his spiritual journey. Accepting the Lord's invitation to "come to a quiet place and get some rest" prepared him for the days when the Spirit would take him through the hard desert places and into an even deeper rest for his soul.

ACCEPTING THE INVITATION TO SOLITUDE

Simpson accepted Christ's invitation to solitude a few months after his conversion. At that time he wrote *A Solemn Covenant*. The writing of the covenant was something that required Simpson's being alone with God and listening to the Spirit's voice within his heart, mind and soul. He set aside a day for fasting and prayer, to contemplate and meditate free of distractions so that the Spirit could affirm, clarify and seal the Father's working within his soul.

As Simpson waited upon God, the Spirit peeled back the layers that covered his heart. He discovered a sinner in the light of God's presence. He acknowledged that he could not trust his own heart. His only recourse was to trust in the grace and mercy of God. He declared that God had subdued his rebellious heart by His love. He concluded his covenant with one single request that revealed his determination and commitment to live his life as a living sacrifice completely in submission to the will of God: "Lord, place me in the circumstances You want. . . . Let Your will be done."[2]

Solitude's initial objective was accomplished. Simpson saw himself in the light of God's presence. He dealt with the issues and things the Spirit had made known. Most of all he drew close to the presence of God and let the Spirit write the Father's script upon his heart. Then he consented to let the sovereign working of God determine the settings, circumstances, events, experiences and people that would be used to bring the Father's will to pass. There would be many similar encounters throughout Simpson's life with Christ.

Solitude was the avenue for settling issues, seeking direction and committing the future to the Father's care. In times of solitude, away from the demands and the distractions of life and ministry, Simpson discovered himself. The discoveries always included glimpses of the inner man he had never seen before. Seeing the inner man, the real A.B. Simpson, in the light of God's presence, this disciple of Jesus Christ continued to make decisions that kept his heart, soul, thoughts, desires, emotions and actions centered upon the Lord.

Silence was solitude's companion in Simpson's preparation for the ministry of preaching and teaching the Word of God. Listening—actively listening—for the Lord's voice was a normal part of the preparation involved in proclaiming God's word. A.E. Thompson notes, "[Simpson's] practice was to hush his spirit and literally cease to think. Then in the silence of his soul he listened for 'the still, small voice.' "[3] Simpson received many of his messages by silently waiting upon the Lord. He was committed to proclaiming the message Christ had laid on his heart. It was a message the people needed to hear. There were times when Simpson found himself waiting until the moment of proclamation before the Lord's message was revealed to him. "For some time the Lord had been withholding the message he was to give . . . until he entered the meeting or a few hours before at the longest."[4]

Does this imply that Simpson neglected study and preparation for his preaching ministry? No, not at all. He continued to study, research and prepare while the Spirit taught him new lessons of waiting and trusting for the message.

The proclamation of God's Word must break through the spiritual blindness that holds people in Satan's grasp. Too much is at stake to risk confusing people with idle words. The Word must flow from messengers who have a message from the Lord. Simpson was very conscious of this as he prepared a new generation of men and women to proclaim the message of Jesus Christ.

On the morning of his seventy-second birthday, A.B. Simpson climbed to the top of the mountain overlooking the campus of the Missionary Training Institute in Nyack, New York. He could see men and women moving across campus, going to and from classes, preparing for ministry to the unreached people of the world. What message did the Lord have for them?

Simpson surrounded himself with the sounds of nature and silently waited upon the Lord. He spent the day silently, expectantly waiting for God. He wanted a new empowerment and a fresh anointing for the work of the Lord. By the end of the day he "had received a renewed call both to studious preparation and prayerful reception of his messages."[5] Chapel provided Simpson with an appropriate opportunity to share a testimony with the student body about the message he had received from the Lord. In doing so, he held forth the example of his own life. It was an example that challenged them to follow him in devoting themselves to their studies. His words also served as an invitation to seek the presence of Jesus and to wait upon the Lord in silent solitude for Christ's message to their hearts.

One by one, they would have to learn what it meant to wait silently upon the Lord. If they were going to take the message of Christ to the unreached the people of their generation, they would need a message from the Lord. The world is filled with confusing words, conflicting principles and sinful expressions that only increase the darkness. It needs the clear, compelling call of God coming from messengers proclaiming the message of Christ in the power of the Spirit to bring light to it.

Waiting upon the Lord in silent solitude was a fundamental spiritual discipline for Simpson. Throughout his life with Christ, times of solitude gave him the opportunity to wait upon God. Getting away from people, demands, expectations and responsibilities allowed him the openness through which the Spirit could impart clarity of thought, heart and soul to him. As Simpson saw himself in the presence of God, the Spirit sealed within his soul the issues that had to be resolved in order for him to continue moving ahead and progressing in the life of faith. Each step with the Lord became the foundation for the next step in a life with Christ that wanted more of God. Explaining Simpson's development in other terms misses the one theme all his recollections, sermons, writings and his diary point to: his deep, passionate commitment to Jesus Christ.[6]

Simpson's heart was the first place for the Lord to accomplish His will. He had to be alone with God and see himself through his Father's eyes. He had to discover the things that were keeping God's will from being accomplished within his life and through his service to Christ. While pastoring the Chestnut Street Presbyterian Church in Louisville, Kentucky, Simpson sensed the Spirit pointing to an area of his life that posed a hindrance to what Christ was seeking to accomplish. The people whom the Spirit was in the process of preparing to receive the good news had to hear the message and needed to experience Christ's love. Listening for the voice of the Lord, Simpson discovered that his commitment to the "regular work" of the ministry was too narrow and restrictive. His priorities had to change. He realized that maintaining the same focus would impede the ministry of salvation. His heart and vision had to expand beyond the boundaries of traditional pastoral responsibilities. He could not limit the expressions of God's grace and mercy to the household of faith. He had to share them with others.

Simpson's initiative united the churches in Louisville in a citywide campaign to reconcile a population still torn apart by the Civil War. The Holy Spirit thrust Simpson beyond the "regular work" of pastoral ministry into the whitened harvest fields. During that time, Simpson's soul was stirred by the preaching of Major Whittle, one of the leading evangelists of the time.

There was something about Whittle, some overtone of power, some fragrance of Christ, some hovering Presence that melted the . . . young Presbyterian minister like a vision of God. A thousand flaws appeared to him, galling, painful, Christ-dishonoring; and worst of all a constant gnawing emptiness within him, a desperate sense of spiritual suffocation. He must have more of God. . . .

When the crisis came . . . he was shut in with God in lonely wrestling like Jacob. . . . His struggle was wholly internal. . . . In the privacy of his own room, with not one soul to understand or sympathize . . . old Adam stood on him and weighed him down till he was crushed as olives are crushed in a press. . . . From that hour he was turned into another man. He would live from that time on, in his own words, "a consecrated, crucified, and Christ-devoted life."[7]

AN AID TO SELF-EXAMINATION

In silent solitude, alone with God, free from the distractions and responsibilities of life and the influence of people, Simpson saw himself in the presence of the Lord. With the Spirit working within his heart and soul, Simpson faced the man in the mirror. Through the Spirit's testimony he saw things about his life, his relationship with Christ and his ministry for the Lord that had to give way before the presence of God. He cast aside his spiritual façade in brokenness before the Lord. Simpson yielded himself to God and, by the Spirit's transforming power, became a new man.

Deep within Simpson's spiritual heritage the Father had planted seeds of missionary outreach. His parents' hearts were touched by the passionate Christian conviction of missionary pioneers like John Geddie, and they eagerly encouraged the development of similar convictions in their children.[8] During his collegiate years at Knox College, Simpson became aware of the potential of united evangelical action. Support for evangelical agencies, mission societies and the Evangelical Alliance was high in the Canadian Presbyterian Church. Missionary outreach was a part of the Knox College campus life.[9]

This was God's time for these seeds to germinate into fruit-bearing ministries. Silently waiting before the Lord in restful solitude provided the conditions that were needed for the Father to do a new work in Simpson's life. Although the path eventually led him further away from the "regular" work of the ministry than he ever imagined, the course and direction of the journey were always in the Father's will. Reaching the lost became the consuming passion of Simpson's soul. He wanted to invest his time, talents and abilities for the Lord in the place that held forth the greatest potential for advancing the kingdom of God.

This encounter with the Lord caused Simpson to review *A Solemn Covenant*, which he had made seventeen years before. As he assessed the progress of his life in Christ, Simpson acknowledged his failures and renewed his commitment and devotion to the Lord. On April 18, 1878, Simpson wrote these words across the covenant:

> Renewed this covenant and dedication amid much temptation and believe that my Father accepts me anew and gives me more than I have dared to ask or think, for Jesus' sake. He has kept His part. My one desire now is power, light, love, souls, Christ's indwelling, and my church's salvation.[10]

While others heralded the success of his pastoral ministry, Simpson recognized his failure before God. He renewed his commitment to live as Jesus' student in obedience to the teachings and the commands of Christ. Relying upon the indwelling presence of the Spirit and the Word revealed to his heart, Simpson followed the example of Jesus. He emulated the practices of his Lord as he walked in fellowship with the Father. He understood that "whoever claims to live in him must walk as Jesus did" (1 John 2:6). Simpson's life echoed the Apostle Paul's invitation: "Follow my example, as I follow the example of Christ" (1 Corinthians 11:1).

The knowledge that there were sheep in other pastures, sheep that needed to be brought into Christ's fold, influenced Simpson's decision to leave Louisville, Kentucky, for New York City. The call to the Thirteenth Street Presbyterian Church would place Simpson near the highest concentration of unreached people in the nation. For Simpson it was a decision the Father would seal in his heart as he sat in quiet solitude before Him. After a week of prayerful meditation and silent waiting upon the Lord, Simpson knew what he had to do.

The Spirit's leading was unmistakable. Simpson was compelled to resign. He knew he must devote himself to serving Christ in the place of God's choosing. In solitude, he discovered what he had to set aside so he could be free to move ahead with the Lord. Simpson explained the process by saying,

> As the light grows deeper and clearer He leads us farther down, and farther on, at once revealing and healing every secret thing that is contrary to His perfect will, as we are able to bear it, and bringing us into perfect conformity to the very nature and life of Christ.[11]

Simpson's pursuit of silence and solitude was influenced by the Quietists. This seventeenth-century movement taught that God is known through the prayer of inward silence after all human thought and feeling is quieted. Their writings challenged Simpson to cultivate the discipline of silence within his soul. Sometime during his Louisville ministry he was influenced by the writings of Madam Guyon and Francis Fenelon.[12] The preface of Harry Verploegh's work, *A.W. Tozer: An Anthology*, identifies the book that influenced Simpson as *A Guide to True Peace, or The Excellency of Inward Spiritual Prayer*.[13]

This book contained what Simpson referred to as "an old medieval message." This message had one central thought: "God was waiting in the depths of my being to talk to me if I would only get still enough to hear His voice."[14] Simpson soon discovered that silently waiting before the Lord was not something that came easily. In his pamphlet *The Power of Stillness*, he described the difficulties he experienced in seeking to be silent before the Lord.

> I began to get still. But I had no sooner commenced than a perfect pandemonium of voices reached my ears, a thousand clamoring notes from without and within, until I could hear nothing but their noise and din. Some of them were my own voice, some of them were my own questions, some of them my own cares, some of them my own prayers. Others were the suggestions of the tempter and the voices of the world's turmoil. Never before did there seem to be so many things to be done, to be said, to be thought; and in every direction I was pulled and pushed and greeted with noisy acclamations and unspeakable unrest. It

seemed necessary for me to listen to some of them, but God said, "Be still, and know I am God."

Then the conflict of thoughts for the morrow and its duties and cares; but God said, "Be still." And then there came the very prayers which my restless heart wanted to press upon Him; but God said, "Be still."

As I listened and slowly learned to obey, and shut my ears to every sound, I found that after a while when the other voices ceased, or I ceased to hear them, there was a still, small voice in the depth of my spirit. As I listened, it became to me the power of prayer, the voice of wisdom and call of duty; and I did not need to think so hard, but that the "still, small voice" of the Holy Spirit in my heart was God's prayer in my secret soul, and God's answer to all my questions.[15]

As Simpson grew in the discipline of silence, it came to have an indispensable place in his ministry of intercession. Consideration of his prayer life reveals the vital role silence played as he sought the Lord in prayer. The discipline of silence also taught him the importance of time in the realization of God's purposes.

We cannot go through life strong and fresh on express trains with ten minutes for lunch. We must have quiet hours, secret places of the Most High, times of waiting on the Lord, when we renew our strength and learn to mount up on wings as eagles and then come back, to run and not be weary and to walk and not faint (see Isaiah 40:31).

The best thing about this stillness is that it gives God a chance to work. "For anyone who enters God's rest also rests from his own work, just as God did from his" (Hebrews 4:10). When we cease from our works, God works in us. When we cease from our thoughts, God's thoughts come into us. When we get still from our restless activity, God works in us both to will and do of His good pleasure, and we have but to work it out.

Let us take His stillness. Let us live in "the shelter of the Most High" (Psalm 91:1). Let us enter into God and His eternal rest. Let us silence the other sounds. Then we can hear "the still, small voice."[16]

There must be time to be alone with the Lord. Our days must not be so hectic that there is no time to be with Christ. The time cannot be hurried. We need time to wait silently, listening for the voice of God. Time is also needed for the Spirit to accomplish the Father's purpose. Spirituality cannot be instantaneously concocted in a fast-paced world. "The law of time is an important factor both in nature and in grace. There are some operations which are instantaneous, but there are many more that require the lapse of time and the process of development."[17]

There are things that God is seeking to accomplish in our lives that we are not yet prepared to receive. Like A.B. Simpson, we must develop the habit, the practice, the discipline, of silently waiting upon God. "There is a cumulative power in waiting prayer to bring the answer and the blessing, breath by breath and moment by moment. God's blessing is too vast and our capacity is too great to be filled in a moment."[18]

In silent solitude, away from the demands, expectations and responsibilities of life and the influence of others, we must wait upon the Lord. His Spirit must open our eyes so we can see ourselves as we really are. We have to know ourselves as He knows us. He will point out the things that have to change. Christ will uncover the things that have to be set aside so that we can continue to grow in the grace of the Lord. Corrective measures have to be taken. Old ways must give way to the new work God wants to accomplish within us. Yesterday's achievements of God's grace are a foundation for the empowering of the Spirit. Today's opportunities for life and service in Jesus flow out of yesterday's service for Christ.

The seasons of solitude that characterized Simpson's relationship with the Lord did not subside with the passing of time. The discipline of solitude became his means for encountering God's sustaining power. Simpson firmly believed that

> God has made each of us, not as self-contained worlds of power and perfection, but simply as vessels waiting to be filled with Him. We are soil to receive His Living Seed and fertilizing streams, and to produce, in union with Him, the fruits of grace.[19]

Accepting Jesus' invitation to "come away by ourselves to a lonely place and rest" (see Mark 6:31) is key to coming to know ourselves and the Lord, who is seeking to fill us with the fullness of

Christ. Solitude ushers us into the Father's presence. In solitude we are able to discover the things that must be set aside so that we can push on toward the fulfillment of God's purpose. Solitude gives the Spirit the freedom to work within us so the Son may be glorified to the praise of the Father.

THE MINISTRY OF THE NIGHT

There is another dimension of solitude that is unknown to many. It is a work of God's redeeming grace that is beyond their realm of experience with Christ. Those who are unwilling to accept the invitation to enter into Jesus' rest are unlikely to appreciate, embrace or even know the ministry A.W. Tozer calls the "ministry of the night."

Others refer to it as "the dark night of the soul." This expression tends to convey a sense of dread or feelings of despair. That in and of itself may cause some to misunderstand this working of God's grace. Connotations such as these could incline the heart to avoid the grace the Father sends to develop our lives in Christ. In his book *Celebration of Discipline*, Richard Foster describes the "ministry of the night":

> When God draws us into the dark night of the soul there is a temptation to blame everyone and everything . . . and to seek release from it. But that is a serious mistake. Recognize the dark night for what it is. Be grateful to God who has lovingly drawn you away from every distraction so that you can see Him. Rather than chafing at it be still and wait.[20]

A.W. Tozer tells us God is seeking to bestow grace upon those who are singled out as the special objects of divine favor. They are honored with discipline that is stricter and suffering that is greater than what others are called upon to endure.[21] The qualifying distinction that causes one to be singled out for this work of grace has to be understood in relation to the individual's receptivity to the things of God.

The heart that is open, responsive and yielded to Christ is strategically positioned to receive the "ministry of the night." It is through this ministry that Christ will build vital elements into one's spiritual character. These elements will play an indispensable role in furthering the cause of Christ within the person's life and then, to others, through their service and ministry for the Lord.

The Spirit will select the tools, circumstances and events God deems necessary to accomplish this special work of grace. Tozer observes,

> Now under the careful treatment of the Holy Spirit your life may become dry, tasteless and to some degree a burden to you. . . .
>
> You will exist by a kind of blind will to live; you will find none of the inward sweetness you enjoyed before. The smile of God will be for the time withdrawn, or at least hidden from your eyes. Then you will learn what faith is; you will find out the hard way, but the only way open to you, that true faith lies in the will, that the joy unspeakable of which the apostle speaks is not itself faith but a slow-ripening fruit of faith; and you will learn that present spiritual joys may come and go as they will without altering your spiritual status or in any way affecting your position as a true child of the heavenly Father. And you will also learn, probably to your astonishment, that it is possible to live in all good conscience before God and men and still feel nothing of the "peace and joy" you hear talked about so much by immature Christians.[22]

The "ministry of the night" cannot be measured in minutes, hours or days. This season of divine favor lasts as long as God deems necessary to accomplish a special work of grace within one's soul. Fulfilling the divine purpose is more important than impatiently measuring the passing of time. Tozer goes on to say,

> Slowly you will discover God's love in your suffering. Your heart will begin to approve the whole thing. You will learn from yourself what all the schools in the world could not teach you—the healing action of faith without supporting pleasure. You will feel and understand the ministry of the night: its power to purify, to detach, to humble, to destroy the fear of death and, what is more important to you at the moment, the fear of life. And you will learn that sometimes pain can do what even joy cannot . . . filling your heart with longing for the peace of heaven.[23]

Those who are not acquainted with the mysterious working of God's grace may not understand the "ministry of the night." They interpret events in terms that describe the obvious. Their attempts to explain things are confined to the natural realm. Their reasoning does not have the spiritual perception that recognizes the spiritual insight, formation and refining of character that is accomplished in the "ministry of the night." It is the work of grace that God accomplishes within the soul that elevates and makes obvious the "ministry of the night."

The failure to recognize this act of grace results in erroneous conclusions and a flawed understanding of what has taken place. This is particularly true in some of the conclusions that are made concerning events in A.B. Simpson's life. Biographers are quick to note that Simpson's relentless pursuit of ministry caused him to push himself too far. As a result he suffered three breakdowns in less than sixteen years. Each time an extended period of rest and recuperation was necessary before he could resume his ministerial responsibilities. They reason that a little less aggressive ambition and a little more moderation would have avoided excesses and spared Simpson from these traumatic illnesses.

If the only thing Simpson did was return to his responsibilities rested, renewed and refreshed, then the natural explanation would suffice. This is a plausible rationalization for those who fail to consider the "ministry of the night." However, it is an inadequate and superficial explanation for what took place in Simpson's heart and service to Christ. Simpson returned from each of these episodes with an enlarged vision for the ministry, a deeper intimacy with Christ and a determination to move ahead into uncharted territory.

Simpson's first encounter with the "ministry of the night" came during his Hamilton, Ontario, pastorate. In July 1869, two years after assuming the Knox Presbyterian Church pastorate, the congregation urged their pastor to take two months off in order to restore his health and vitality. Simpson agreed to accept the proposal on the condition that one month would be more than sufficient.[24] The stage was set. The brief sabbatical only served to forestall the inevitable. Less than two years later Simpson was physically and emotionally depleted. He needed a break from ministerial responsibilities. Everyone agreed that it would be beneficial for him to spend the summer in Europe.

Simpson described the way he was feeling in a letter to his wife Margaret: "As to the effect of the air—I cannot begin to tell you how exhilarating it has been, and how much better I feel after the stupid dullness of the past months."[25] The words "stupid dullness" reveal the state of Simpson's mind, heart and spiritual vitality. His vibrancy had been stripped away. Simpson was walking through the "ministry of the night." God was preparing His servant, strategically positioning and getting him ready for the missionary movement that would be entrusted to him in the future.

The spiritual insight that came to Simpson during this "ministry of the night" nourished the seeds of missionary involvement already residing within his heart. His understanding of missions would take on new dimensions as he confronted the undeniable truth about the Old World. It was a truth he did not expect to encounter. He went anticipating an inspirational tour of Europe but encountered something different. He describes what he saw in a letter to Margaret: "There is a sad corruption and rottenness in the moral and social life of these countries."[26]

To Simpson, the prospect of spiritual renewal beginning in Europe and spreading in a missionary movement to the unreached people of the world was highly unlikely. He had little reason to believe that a new "reformation" could ever spawn from those social and moral conditions. For the first time, the young Canadian pastor came face-to-face with radical evil in the world, evil unlike anything he had ever encountered. Nothing could have prepared him for what he saw in Europe.

Europe's moral condition and religious atmosphere did not inspire Simpson's confidence in the Church's ability to influence European society. He reluctantly concluded that hope would have to come from someplace else. God would have to raise up people from another place to share the gospel with the unreached people of the world. Europe, the birthplace of the Reformation, needed spiritual renewal. Simpson concluded that the hope would have to come from the New World. "The Old World is going fast to the devil and I look with hope to the New."[27]

The hope must come from the New World. Instead of looking to someone else, hope has to come from us. Instead of waiting for others to take the lead, we must give ourselves anew to every effort and means possible to advance the gospel of Christ. This is the prevailing spiritual insight that emerged within Simpson's heart and mind through this "ministry of the night." He would see missions, the lost, the believers' responsibilities and the opportunities to advance Christ's kingdom in a new light and with a sense of urgency unlike anything he had ever known before. Hope for the spiritual renewal of Europe and the unreached peoples of the world would have to come from the West. Little did Simpson realize that in God's time, he would play a key role in global evangelization.

A foreshadowing of this role came after his time in Europe. While serving in Louisville, Kentucky, God once again favored Simpson with the "ministry of the night." It was time for Simpson to discover three necessary and primary truths that would affect the rest of his life, ministry and walk with Christ. First, he would learn that the Spirit-filled life is absolutely necessary to the divine empowerment for ministry. The place of personal yieldedness and submission to Christ would be engraved upon his heart. Second, a vision for missions, for taking the gospel of Christ to the unreached masses, would begin to blaze within his soul. Finally, he would come to realize that he had to be free to serve in the place of greatest opportunity.

This time Simpson would experience two distinctive episodes of the "ministry of the night." The first came in the midst of what seemed to be a successful ministry. Everything appeared to be fine. Evidence of God's blessing seemed to be everywhere. The Chestnut Street Presbyterian Church was experiencing unprecedented growth, and Simpson was a key catalyst in a citywide evangelistic crusade. Seeing the flood of spiritual renewal sweeping through the city and witnessing people respond to the message of salvation fueled the vision growing within his heart.

Within Simpson's heart a totally different set of dynamics was coming into play. The vision was beyond the realm of human endeavor. It was greater than his experience or abilities. Accomplishing it would take more than strategic planning, unwavering dedication and strenuous service for Christ. Prayerful reflection, thoughtful consideration and careful examination of his own life brought Simpson to a firm, undeniable conclusion: The realization of his vision would take something more, something greater than he had to give.

As Simpson interacted with evangelist Major Whittle and the gifted song leader Philip P. Bliss and witnessed what Christ was accomplishing through their service, turmoil continued to grow within him. This widely respected and successful church and community leader sensed a deepening dissatisfaction within his own soul. He became increasingly convinced that the depth of his own spiritual life was inadequate. He felt the need for a touch from the Lord to revitalize his life and ministry. The touch he needed was the indwelling of the Holy Spirit.[28]

In the months that followed, the quest to fill the hunger and longing within Simpson's soul took many shapes and forms. The journey passed through rocky places and dry desert valleys. A variety of people, circumstances and events were used by God to bring Simpson to the point of complete and total submission to the person and the will of Jesus Christ. Simpson recalls the journey with terms that affirm that he was indeed in the midst of a "ministry of the night":

> I look back with unutterable gratitude to the lonely and sorrowful night when, mistaken in many things and imperfect in all, and not knowing that it would be death in the most literal sense before the morning light, my heart's first full consecration was made. . . . And if God has been pleased to make my life in any measure a little temple for His indwelling and for His glory, and if He ever shall be pleased to use me in any fuller measure, it has been because of that hour, and it will be still in the measure in which that hour is made the key-note of a consecrated, crucified, and Christ-devoted life.[29]

Simpson's words testify to the crucial turning point—the moment of complete surrender and total consecration made in his life. Dissatisfaction gave way to a sense of Christ's indwelling and the Spirit's empowerment for life and ministry. Simpson's comments on the conscious realization of Christ's presence living within him reveal a basic, fundamental change in his relationship with the Lord. "Christ has been given ownership of the house. Jesus no longer occupies part of the house. He is the proprietor who is taking care of me and using me."[30]

This marked a new beginning in Simpson's life with Christ. It was the beginning of what he called the sanctified life. He ardently asserted that sanctification is not self-improvement, nor is it some spiritual height Christians are able to attain. To him it was nothing less than the transforming life of Christ living within the believer, the inflow of Christ's life, perfection and purity into the believer's life.

> There is a great difference between our receiving power from the Holy Ghost and our receiving the Holy Ghost as our power. In the latter case we are as insignificant and insufficient as ever, and it is the Person who dwells within us who possesses and exercises all the gifts and powers of our ministry, and only as we abide in Him and He works in us are we able to exercise this power.[31]

There is a distinctive difference between empowering and possessing. Many want the Lord's empowering without Christ's possessing. At best, this reflects spiritual immaturity coupled with a lack of understanding. It underscores the need for spiritual insight, development and understanding. At its worst, the desire for empowerment without possession is a reflection of Simon the Sorcerer's heart— "Give me also this ability so that everyone on whom I lay my hands may receive the Holy Spirit" (Acts 8:19). This is the epitome of sinfulness. It is a carnal expression which seeks to subjugate the divine to the whims of human desire.

In the midst of the "ministry of the night" he experienced during this time, Simpson recognized his own spiritual ignorance and lack of understanding concerning the Spirit-filled life. He confessed his misguided devotion and the change Christ brought to his heart in these words:

> Once it was the blessing,
> Now it is the Lord;
> Once it was the feeling,
> Now it is His Word.
>
> Once His gifts I wanted,
> Now the Giver own.

Once I sought for healing,
Now Himself alone.

Once 'twas painful trying,
Now it's perfect trust.
Once a half salvation,
Now the uttermost!

Once 'twas ceaseless holding,
Now He holds me fast.
Once 'twas constant drifting,
Now my anchor's cast.

Once 'twas busy planning,
Now it's trustful prayer.
Once 'twas anxious caring,
Now He has the care.

Once 'twas what I wanted,
Now what Jesus says.
Once 'twas constant asking,
Now it's ceaseless praise.

Once it was my working,
His it hence shall be.
Once I tried to use Him,
Now He uses me.

Once the power I wanted,
Now the Mighty One.
Once for self I labored,
Now for Him alone.

Once I hoped for Jesus,
Now I know He's mine.
Once my lamps were dying,
Now they brightly shine.

Once for death I waited,
Now His coming hail.
And my hopes are anchored
Safe within the veil.

All in all forever,
Jesus will I sing.

Everything in Jesus,
And Jesus everything.[32]

These lyrics express Simpson's longing for a life of unbroken communion and fellowship with the Lord. They describe and call for a relationship with the living Christ as the sole proprietor of his soul. Submission and trust are indispensable elements in the life surrendered to Christ. For Simpson, they were elements that would soon be put to the test.

Conflicting ideas, expectations and plans concerning the construction of a new church in Louisville mired the Chestnut Street congregation in conflict that threatened both the viability of the building program and of Simpson's vision for a church with an outward-focused ministry. Simpson was stymied. He did not know which way to turn. He needed guidance, direction and wisdom on how to resolve the matter. He decided to consult with D.L. Moody in the hopes that perhaps Moody would have the words he needed to hear. The evening Simpson arrived in Chicago, Moody was conducting a tent meeting. Simpson sat down and listened. People in the crowd were sharing words of testimony. A minister stood to speak. Tears streamed down his cheeks as, in a broken voice, he offered a testimony for the Lord: "Friends, I came here to get something from the meeting; but God took me out alone with Him, and I have had such a sight of Jesus that I will never need anybody or anything again."[33]

The testimony cut to the very core of Simpson's heart. Instead of trusting the Lord, he had been letting the difficulties over the new church building consume him. Waiting upon the Lord had been pushed aside in favor of seeking counsel from others. Simpson never consulted with Moody.

> I took the train the next morning for home. As I entered my office, the face of Jesus was awaiting there to receive me; and there came such a flood of His presence and grace and His glory that it seemed I could say, "I have had such a vision of Jesus that it seems as if I could never fear again."[34]

This incident serves to illustrate the progressive nature of the Spirit-filled life. Opportunities to affirm and refine our trust, submission and yieldedness to the Lord are continually presented to us as Christ's children. They serve to remind us of areas in our relationships with God where trust has the potential to grow. This potential for growing deeper and drawing closer to Jesus will be realized as we confess our shortcomings and continue on in our lives with Him.

LEARNING YIELDEDNESS

A.B. Simpson never viewed sanctification as an instantaneous attainment. To him, sanctification was an ongoing, progressive experience flowing out of our commitment to and relationship with Jesus Christ. "He is the Author and the Finisher of our faith, and the true attitude of the consecrated heart is that of a constant yielding and constant receiving. This . . . gives boundless scope to our spiritual progress."[35]

Simpson's spiritual journey would soon encounter uncharted territory. The seeds of missionary awareness sown in his heart through the influence of his parents, the missionary emphasis of the Canadian Presbyterian Church and the missions promotion and fervor that was a part of the atmosphere and campus life at Knox College were germinating within Simpson's soul.

The success of the evangelistic outreach in Louisville provided the right conditions for those seeds to blossom in Simpson's life. Involvement in the citywide evangelistic crusade seeking the salvation of the unreached masses positioned his heart to receive a word from the Lord. This word would come in the form of a dream. It was a dream that called for a response that would require a deeper level of yieldedness to Christ. No words were spoken; in the dream there was only a visual image of multitudes of people with anguished, tormented expressions on their faces. The vision communicated a clear and compelling message: These people are perishing without the hope of salvation. With the message came the obvious application: What will you do about it? What role will you play in bringing them the message of salvation, the hope of Jesus Christ?

Simpson vividly remembered the vision and the message he received from the Lord.

> I was awakened one night from sleep, trembling with a strange and solemn sense of God's overshadowing power, and on my soul was burning the remembrance of a strange dream through which I had come. It seemed to me that I was sitting in a vast auditorium, and millions of people were sitting around me. All the Christians in the world seemed to be there, and on the platform was a great multitude of faces and forms. They seemed to be mostly Chinese. They were not speaking, but in mute anguish were wringing their hands, and their faces wore an expression that I can never forget. I had not been thinking of the Chinese or the heathen world; but as I awoke with that vision on my mind, I did tremble with the Holy Spirit, and I threw myself on my knees and every fiber of my being answered, "Yes, Lord, I will go."[36]

These words of commitment marked the opening of a new phase of Simpson's life in and service to Jesus Christ. In that moment "missions" was born within Simpson's soul. Yieldedness to Christ opened the door to an opportunity that would eclipse everything he had ever known. In just a matter of time a new missionary movement focusing on the people living beyond the gospel's reach would emerge. It would lead to the founding of the first Bible college in America to train and equip believers for service to Christ at home and abroad. Everything that has been accomplished for Christ throughout the world under the banner of The Christian and Missionary Alliance in the past, and everything that will be accomplished in the future, flows from this decisive moment as Simpson, in trustful yieldedness and submission, said, "Yes, Lord, I will go."

Through the "ministry of the night" Christ was positioning and preparing Simpson for the ministry that would be entrusted to him. He was committed to the Spirit-filled life, a life of sanctification, in which the Spirit's empowerment enables the believer to accomplish Christ's work. Christ's indwelling presence quenched Simpson's thirst and satisfied the hunger of his soul. His heart, vision and arms were open to the unreached people of the world. The servant was willing to go.

It was time for another "ministry of the night" that would release him to a place of service that would strategically position
him to launch the new missionary movement. Simpson would
find that the necessary release would come with a price.

The circumstances for Simpson's next experience of the "ministry of the night" were similar to what he had experienced in Ontario. He suffered another physical and emotional collapse. Totally
and completely expended, he stepped aside from all pastoral duties
and ministerial responsibilities for an extended period of rest and
recuperation. He spent five months convalescing in Clifton Springs,
New York, during which time he was afforded the opportunity to
assess his relationship with Christ. He returned to Louisville and re-
sumed his pastoral responsibilities with a renewed passion and
commitment to the vision burning within his soul. The text for his
first message upon his return was Philippians 3:13-14. It was

> . . . the language of a man making a new start in life, turning
> from the past as a disappointment and almost a failure to the
> pursuit of a better future than he has yet attained. And when we
> remember that the man who uses this language was no less than
> Paul, and that it was spoken not at the beginning but almost at
> the close of his career, and that after . . . that wondrous history
> recorded in the Acts, and embodied in the Epistles, a life grand
> enough to make up the lives of a thousand ordinary heroes, we
> could well afford to lie down with him in the dust and say, "I
> have not attained: but this one thing I do, forgetting the things
> that are behind, and reaching forth unto those things that are
> before, I press toward the mark for the prize of the high calling of
> God in Jesus Christ."[37]

The turmoil of Simpson's personal life, conflicts within the
church, a changing philosophy of ministry and the creative tension
spawned by the enlarged vision growing within his soul were vital
issues during the "ministry of the night" that Simpson endured.

In Simpson's mind, nothing could stand in the way of advancing
the gospel. The message of Christ must be taken to the unreached
people of the world. Evangelism at home and missions abroad became the priorities of Simpson's life and ministry. He would not
surrender his convictions that economical, utilitarian facilities

freed the Church to invest their resources into ministries directly promoting the salvation of the lost. Nor would Simpson abandon his belief that needless indebtedness impaired the gospel's advance. God's kingdom could not afford the luxury of inwardly focused congregations. Christ's call was to be the salt and the light of the world. Simpson unashamedly believed that the gospel of the kingdom had to be preached in the whole world as a testimony to the nations, and then the end would come (see Matthew 24:14). He avowed that the Church could hasten the Lord's return through evangelism and missions to the unreached people of the world.

Simpson's various experiences with the "ministry of the night" were preparing him for his life's work. As a result of the first instance of the "ministry of the night," Simpson recognized that the West, the New World, would play a prominent role in global evangelization. After the second experience, he embraced the sanctified life, a life lived in the presence and power of the Spirit under the Lordship of Jesus Christ. He learned that only through the Spirit's empowerment could the work of Christ be accomplished. From the third instance, he understood that the Church must be free to seize the moment and walk through new doors of opportunity. As Christ's servant he had to be free to follow the Lord's leading. Simpson emerged from the "ministry of the night" determined to follow Christ's leading no matter where the path would lead.

In a matter of months the path took him to New York City. The potential for reaching people for Christ through evangelistic outreach and missionary enterprises was greater than anything Simpson had ever known. The city was a microcosm of the world. Its ethnic diversity coupled with the seemingly endless stream of immigrants pouring through Ellis Island represented the global harvest field.

Those were days of unparalleled opportunity. Simpson sought to mobilize his congregation, the Thirteenth Street Presbyterian Church, for aggressive evangelistic outreach. He launched the publication of an illustrated missionary magazine, *The Gospel in All Lands,* to raise missions awareness in North America and to advocate an unprecedented effort by all denominations to recruit and deploy missionaries throughout the world. He also invested a significant portion of his time in ministering to the immigrants seeking a new way of life. If he reached them for Jesus, perhaps the testimony of their newfound life in Christ would travel across the Atlantic to Europe and effect the salvation of family members and friends on the European continent.

It was just a matter of time before the relentless pace of such an exhausting ministerial schedule, personal concerns within his family and dealing with previously undisclosed sensitive issues within the Church ushered Simpson into one final encounter of God's grace through the "ministry of the night." A broken, empty vessel was about to experience a new dimension of God's grace. Christ's touch upon Simpson's life guided him into an encounter with the sufficiency of Jesus Christ. God was going to use the pain of bodily affliction and adversity to introduce A.B. Simpson to the healing ministry of Jesus Christ.

The seeds for this ministry of grace were planted in Simpson's heart through a dramatic incident that occurred during his pastoral ministry in Louisville. There was nothing the physicians could do for a certain young man. It was only a matter of time. His mother, a devout Christian, called for Simpson and asked him to pray for her son. Simpson recalls, "As I prayed I was led to ask not for his healing but that he might recover long enough to let his mother know that he was saved."[38] To everyone's surprise the young man regained consciousness. In a relatively short period of time he completely recovered from the illness. Simpson recalls his response to the man's testimony of God's grace:

> The impression produced by that incident never left me. Soon afterward I attempted to take the Lord as my Healer. For a while, as long as I trusted Him, He sustained me wonderfully. But . . . I abandoned my position of simple dependence on God alone and floundered and stumbled for years. But as I heard of isolated cases of miraculous healings, I never dared to doubt them or question that God did sometimes so heal. For myself, however, the truth had no really practical or effectual power, for I never could feel that I had any clear authority in a given case of need to trust myself to Him.[39]

THE HEALING CHRIST

Simpson was about to find himself in a position where he needed to trust Christ as his healer. His diary entries record comments that suggest he knew his health was failing. January 4, 1880, "Very tired and worn—but held to much prayer." Eight days later, January 12, "Tired." The entry for February 1, "Unwell all day. Broken down much."[40] The clock was ticking. Strength and vitality were rapidly diminishing. Simpson was unable to continue juggling all the demands, commitments and responsibilities he had assumed in New York City. He forestalled the inevitable by suspending publication of the June edition of *The Gospel in All Lands* and relinquishing the publishing and managing responsibilities to Eugene R. Smith.

The day of grace was coming as the "ministry of the night" loomed before him. Simpson confessed, "I struggled through my work most of the time. . . . It usually took me until Wednesday to get over the effects of the Sunday sermon."[41] The pace could not continue. Simpson's physician prescribed a period of relaxation and a change of climate, suggesting the warm waters of Saratoga Springs, New York, which were known to have beneficial medicinal effects. Simpson thought that perhaps they would prove beneficial to him as well. But it was not the warm subterranean spring water that he needed. He needed nothing less than the healing power of the Living Water.

One afternoon as Simpson wandered through the campground he was staying in, he happened to overhear the sound of singing in the distance. Curiosity caused him to move closer. He stood in the distance listening to the singing.

> My Jesus is the Lord of lords:
> No man can work like Him. . . .
> No man can work like Him . . .
> No man can work like Him.[42]

The chorus resounded in Simpson's mind over and over again. As the Fisk University Jubilee Singers lifted their voices in praise to God, Simpson experienced a special sense of Christ's presence. The words of the song

> . . . fell upon me like a spell. It fascinated me. It seemed like a
> voice from heaven. It possessed my whole being. I took Jesus to

be my Lord of lords and to work in my behalf. I knew not how much it all meant. But I took Him in the dark and went forth from that rude, old-fashioned service, remembering nothing else, but strangely lifted up forevermore.[43]

Christ used the chorus to lift Simpson's heart and to prepare the way for a new encounter with God's grace. A few weeks later, he took his family to Old Orchard Beach, Maine. During the time there he heard a number of people give testimony to the healing power of Christ. They declared that the Lord had healed them of sickness and affliction. Simpson recalled his response to their words of testimony:

These testimonies drove me to my Bible. I determined that I must settle the matter one way or the other. I am glad I did not go to man. At Jesus' feet, alone, with my Bible open and with no one to help or guide me, I became convinced that this was part of Christ's glorious gospel for a sinful and suffering world—the purchase of His blessed cross for all who would believe and receive His Word.

That was enough. I could not believe this and then refuse to take it for myself. I felt I dare not hold any truth in God's Word as a mere theory or teach to others what I had not personally proved. And so one Friday afternoon at 3 o'clock, I went out into the silent pine woods. There I raised my right hand to heaven and in view of the judgment day, I made to God, as if I had seen Him there before me face to face, these three eternal pledges:

1. *As I shall meet Thee in that day, I solemnly accept this truth as part of Thy Word and the gospel of Christ. Thou helping me, I shall never question it until I meet Thee there.*

2. *As I shall meet Thee in that day, I take the Lord Jesus as my physical life for all the needs of my body until my life work is done. Thou helping me, I shall never doubt that Thou dost so become my life and strength from this moment and wilt keep me under all circumstances until Thy blessed coming and until Thy will for me is perfectly fulfilled.*

3. *As I shall meet Thee in that day, I solemnly agree to use this blessing for Thy glory and the good of others. I agree to speak of it or minister in connection with it in any way in which Thou mayest call me or others may need me in the future.*[44]

That day marked Simpson's entry into a new dimension of life in Christ. With an open heart and mind he searched the Scriptures. In quiet solitude he discovered the sufficiency of Christ for the body. He experienced the Lord's healing power. "I knew that something was done. Every fiber of my soul was tingling with a sense of God's presence."[45] From that day forward Simpson lived in dependence upon the Lord for his physical needs.

The days that followed brought numerous tests of his trust in Christ the Healer. Satan sought to sow seeds of doubt and plant subtle suggestions in an effort to dissuade Simpson's faith. Scorn and ridicule were hurled by those who could not embrace the ministry of healing. Simpson never wavered. He advocated the ministry of healing as prescribed in the epistle of James as a legitimate and valid ministry of the Church for our day. The sick "should call the elders of the church to pray over him and anoint him with oil in the name of the Lord. And the prayer offered in faith will make the sick person well; the Lord will raise him up. If he has sinned, he will be forgiven" (James 5:14-15).

In the face of all the opposition Simpson encountered, one undeniable fact remained: Christ's healing touch transformed his life. He experienced a supernatural touch upon his life granting him physical strength and vitality to minister and serve in the name of the Lord. It was a message that had to be shared.

> I returned to my work. . . . [W]ith deep gratitude to God I can truly say, hundreds being my witnesses, that for many years I have been permitted to labor for the dear Lord in summer's heat or winter's cold without interruption, without a single season of protracted rest and with increasing comfort, strength and delight. Life has had for me a zest, and labor an exhilaration that I never knew in the freshest days of my childhood.[46]

A.B. Simpson became a proponent of the ministry of healing. Christ the Savior, Sanctifier and Coming King of Simpson's life became also Christ his Healer. The ministry of healing continues to be an Alliance distinctive.

The disciplines of silence and solitude played a vital role in Simpson's spiritual formation, development and lifelong ministry. Christ's invitation to come away with Him to a quiet place of rest ushered Simpson into a life of total commitment to his Lord. It was a commitment that would grow stronger, broader and deeper as Simpson progressed, matured and grew in the life of Christ. Even in the twilight days of his life, Simpson stepped away from people and responsibilities to places of silent solitude with the Lord.

The "ministry of the night" was a gift of God's grace that was an indispensable element in A.B. Simpson's spiritual and personal growth. The "ministry of the night" coincided with crisis moments in Simpson's spiritual journey. Each encounter opened a new dimension of life with Christ. As Simpson comprehended the significance of the truth God's grace had made known to his heart and mind in the midnight hour, he incorporated that truth into his life and his ministry. Christ as Sanctifier, the empowering of the Spirit for life and service, came to Simpson through the "ministry of the night." The same can be said for his commitment to his driving determination to take the gospel to the unreached people of the world. He could not be fettered by tradition or bound by conventional expectations. Simpson had to be free to seize the moment of opportunity and share the hope of Christ with unreached people at home and abroad. Also, if it were not for the "ministry of the night," The Christian and Missionary Alliance would not know the grace of the Lord's touch through the ministry of healing.

A.B. Simpson looked upon the "ministry of the night" as a part of the life Christ had called him to. It was not something to be shunned, but was to be embraced and understood as something that God had chosen to give because Christ's love seeks to accomplish God's very best in the lives of all Christians.

> In the beginning of this life of faith God gave me a vision which to me was a symbol of the kind of life to which He had called me. In this dream a little sailboat was passing down a rapid stream, tossed by the winds and driven by the rapids. Every moment it seemed as if it must be dashed upon the rocks and crushed, yet it was preserved in some mysterious way and carried through all perils. Upon the sails of the little ship was plainly painted the name of the vessel in one Latin word, *Angustiae,* meaning "Hard Places." Through this simple dream the Lord seemed to fortify me for the trials and testings that were ahead, and to prepare me

for a life's voyage which was to be far from a smooth one, but through which God's grace would always carry me in triumph.[47]

The "ministry of the night" introduced Simpson to the working of God's grace and mercy in ways that brought him closer to the heart of God. He experienced a joy and a closeness that is never known by those who confine their walk with Christ to the familiar, safe places.

CONSIDERATIONS FOR YOUR SPIRITUAL DEVELOPMENT

Places to go, things to do, appointments to meet, schedules to keep—activities and commitments fill our days with a seemingly endless list of responsibilities. There is far more to do than there is time to do it. Many people are living on the verge of exhaustion, and the margins that are supposed to provide a safe buffer have all but disappeared. If there was ever a time when God's people needed to embrace the discipline of solitude, it is today.

Stepping back from the responsibilities of life and ministry to have uninterrupted time with Christ is essential to our spiritual formation and vitality. Tromping off to another conference, seminar or workshop filled with activity is not solitude. The opportunity to participate in solitude may come through Jesus' invitation, "Come with me by yourselves to a quiet place and get some rest" (Mark 6:31).

● ● ● ● ● ● ● ● ● ● ● *Application*

1. Have you ever responded to Jesus' invitation to step away and be alone with Him? If so, describe the setting, the atmosphere. Did you encounter any distractions? If so, how did you overcome the distractions? Do you recall how the Lord met you and what Christ affirmed to your heart?
2. Are you planning to accept Jesus' invitation to solitude again? How would you like Jesus to meet you?

3. Do you or are you planning to practice solitude on a regular basis? If so, describe the benefits solitude offers.

    The "ministry of the night" or the "dark night of the soul" is the second dimension of solitude. A.W. Tozer described it as the solitude God's loving grace imposes upon those who are singled out as the special objects of divine favor. The "ministry of the night" may involve loneliness, pain and suffering. Instead of seeking to remove ourselves from the ministry, we need to embrace it and through the process of embracing it discover the sufficiency of God's grace and presence.

4. Is it possible to misinterpret adversity as an indication of God's chastisement instead of seeing it as a sign of God's grace? Why do you suppose this happens?

5. If God chooses to further your spiritual development through the things that are involved in the "dark night of the soul," will you joyfully embrace it?

6. Does it seem strange to you that God would choose to develop spiritual character in our lives in this way? Why or why not?

LIVING FOR THE LORD'S PLEASURE
Practicing *Secrecy*

"Dare to Compare," "Best Value, Lowest Price" and "The Comfort You Deserve—The Luxury You Can Afford" are just a few of the advertising slogans that are currently vying for our attention. Radio, television, newspaper and magazine advertising attempts to capture our imagination, arouse our curiosity and lure us into the marketplace. "Compare, compare, compare" appears to be the favorite concept in advertising.

Cleverly designed commercials featuring everything from dancing blue lights to smiley faces wearing work gloves and construction hats ingrain a comparative spirit within the fabric of our culture. Comparisons are everywhere. Compare the price, the selection, the value, the quality, the satisfaction, the service before and after the sale and everything and anything else you can think of.

No one questions the value of comparison or suggests that comparisons shouldn't be made. Comparing can keep us from making costly mistakes and can help us avoid unnecessary blunders. It can play a beneficial role in the prudent use of our resources and in making wise choices.

Unfortunately, there is another side to comparison. It is a side that distorts reality and has devastating consequences. When the value, acceptance, potential and dignity of a person are determined by comparison, we've entered into a process, accepted a premise and embraced a way of ascertaining value that is contrary to the heart of God. We place ourselves in an adversarial role with the Creator and begin to act in a way that is contrary to the purpose and person of Jesus Christ.

Sometimes Christians tend to overlook the fact that the heart and arms of Jesus are willing and ready to receive anyone who comes to Him. Instead of embracing God's acceptance in Jesus Christ and passing it on to others unconditionally, there is a tendency to position ourselves to impress others. Sometimes we try to gain others' acceptance and approval so we can move in their circles. The "impression factor" can become a dominating force in a person's life. Instead of living life to please the Lord, the thoughts, motives and intentions of the heart are given over to doing things to impress and gain the approval of other people. Those who do so find that "approval addiction"—living in bondage to what others think of them[1]—becomes a controlling force in their lives.

The insidious nature of approval addiction inevitably results in comparisons that have no other purpose than to make us look good. These comparisons have nothing to do with potential, opportunity, talent, ability or the obstacles encountered or contended with along the way. They have everything to do with results. Inevitably we compare ourselves with someone whose accomplishments are not as impressive. If, per chance, the comparison involves someone with a superior performance, we give an explanation that diminishes the significance of their accomplishments while noting how our performance was hindered by extenuating factors. In either case the rationalization always makes us look good.

Is this what Christian living is about—making ourselves look good compared to others? Is this what Christ died to accomplish in the lives of those who follow and serve Him? Are results immersed in the impression factor in order to satisfy an approval addiction the real concern of Christ's kingdom? No. Jesus' concern is whether the kingdom is present in reborn hearts and remade relationships.[2]

MEASURING IN TERMS OF CALVARY

One of A.B. Simpson's primary concerns was the presence of Christ's kingdom in the hearts and lives of His people. Simpson felt it should permeate their relationships with God, with one another and with those living outside the realm of God's redeeming grace. He knew that the worth of a soul and the value of life could only be measured in terms of Calvary: the place where God the Son gave Himself to redeem the people of every culture and language to the glory of God the Father. The vision burning deep within Simpson's heart was to know Christ and to make Him known to the unreached people of the world.

Simpson was not concerned with winning the approval of men. His sole ambition was to introduce all kinds of people to the Savior. It was Simpson's opinion, and rightly so, that impressing people and religious posturing belong to people who are concerned with lesser things.

There is a spiritual discipline that frees us from approval addiction and the impression factor. It is a spiritual discipline Jesus introduced to the multitudes in the Sermon on the Mount. This discipline is called secrecy. It is a discipline Jesus watched religious exhibitionists trample under their feet in their attempts to impress people with their spirituality.

In the Sermon on the Mount, Jesus shares a spiritual principle for anyone thinking about trying to impress others: "Be careful not to do your 'acts of righteousness' before men, to be seen by them" (Matthew 6:1). Jesus tells us to make sure we avoid practicing our faith in ways that call attention to what we are doing. Faith, service and ministry are not about impressing people. They are about fulfilling the Savior's purpose and bringing joy to God's heart. Jesus cautions us to avoid stepping into the snare of trying to win men's praise.

The seriousness with which Jesus expects His followers to take this spiritual principle and apply it to their daily lives can be found in the statement Jesus makes about the consequences awaiting those who want others' approval. "If you do, you will have no reward from your Father in heaven" (6:1). There is a choice to make. Forfeiting the Father's reward is the price for the momentary fix approval addiction brings. When the attention fades and the act of righteousness is only a distant memory, the eternal satisfaction of hearing the words, "Well done, good and faithful servant!" (25:23) will never be heard.

Service for Christ that is true and acceptable to God has nothing to do with carefully calculated actions that are designed to impress other people or call attention to ourselves. These things are merely a carnal display of self-glorification masquerading as a momentary expression of spirituality parading across the stage. No matter how these things are practiced, the intention is always the same: "Look at me! Look at me!"

How can we point people to the Savior while we are shouting, "Look at me! Look at me!"? By standing in the spotlight, we obscure Jesus from the view of people who need Him. It also hinders the work of God in the lives of those who attempt to usurp the attention.

The last thing A.B. Simpson wanted was to live and serve in a way that obscured Jesus from view. He took to heart the three practical illustrations concerning giving, fasting and prayer that Jesus shared with the people. Jesus' words, "[Do it] in secret. Then your Father, who sees what is done in secret, will reward you" (Matthew 6:4), defined Simpson's life and ministry.

It is not that the things Simpson did would never become known. It meant that his service and ministry to Christ was for the Lord's approval and the Father's pleasure. Impressing others, doing or not doing the things that made for the approval of men, had no place in Simpson's life with Christ. Dallas Willard observes that secrecy teaches us to be content with God's approval. Our "acts of righteousness" and the practice of our faith are a service to God that is not filtered through other people.[3] The discipline of secrecy calls us to follow Christ in living a life of faith that is not tarnished by things that solicit the praise or the approval of others.

Christ's approval is what mattered to A.B. Simpson. His life and ministry echo the words of the Apostle Paul: "If I were still trying to please men, I would not be a servant of Christ" (Galatians 1:10). Simpson was content to follow Jesus without gaining the approval of others. Although he respected the counsel and wisdom of godly men, the final arbiter was the Word of the Lord to his heart, the will of God for his life and the direction the Spirit impressed upon his soul.

When Simpson sensed the Spirit directing him to pursue a path others were not willing to embrace or follow, he respected their positions, but he served the Lord. A man who lives a life of faith must move ahead with the mind of Christ and the leading of the Spirit.

The first opportunity Simpson may have had to begin embracing the discipline of secrecy came before he even began to prepare for ministry. Possessing only the call of God to a life of pastoral ministry and the assurance of his parents' blessing, Simpson faced a financial dilemma. Neither he nor his family had the financial resources to pay for college. Seeking funding for the venture, Simpson took a position as a public school teacher. As a fifteen-year-old boy, not even old enough to shave, he stood before a class of forty people. While other young men sought jobs as hired farmhands, Simpson became a teacher in a classroom where nearly a fourth of the students were grown men and women old enough to be his parents. The prospect of a teen gaining such a position seems contrary to conventional wisdom. Certainly there were those who took issue with entrusting Simpson with the position and cautioned against it. But Simpson realized the value this position would have in helping prepare him for the rigorous occupation of a pastor.

Contending with the expectations of others came into play again with Simpson's graduation from Knox College. Many expressed their opinions about where this aspiring young man should serve. All his professors and friends urged him to accept a call to serve a church that offered a comfortable place of ministry. They reasoned that he would have the opportunity to develop his pastoral skills. Their counsel made sense—no one could argue with the logic or the wisdom of their reasoning. But Simpson sensed the Spirit directing him to accept the call to serve in a more difficult place. Reflecting on the experience some time later, he said, "[By] an impulse, which I now believe to have been, at least indirectly, from God . . . my early ministry was developed . . . by the grace of God, through the necessities of this difficult position."[4]

"Difficult" is an understatement! In accepting the call to serve the Knox Presbyterian Church, Simpson assumed the pastoral leadership of a church facing hard times. The turmoil surrounding his predecessor's resignation eighteen months before Simpson's arrival was continuing to drain the spiritual vitality from the congregation. A thirty-percent decline in membership was accompanied by a fifty-percent decrease in financial support.[5]

Contrary to the conventional wisdom about an appropriate place to begin one's ministry, the Lord's desire was to place Simpson in a position where the formative years of his ministry would be fashioned and shaped by less-than-comfortable service. Early on Simpson learned that it is not the presence or absence of numbers that matters. The thing that is precious and valuable in the sight of God is the presence of Christ's kingdom in the hearts and relationships of people. Faith, prayer, sacrifice and service proved to be vital elements in bringing spiritual renewal and growth to the Knox Church congregation. The key that initiated the process was Simpson's desire to please the Lord by accepting the opportunity to serve in the harder place, the place others counseled him against considering.

Practicing the discipline of secrecy means being true to the call of God upon your life and true to yourself by following both the vision and the burden of ministry the Lord gives to you. The life of Christ is not about impressing people. It is about serving the Lord.

Even as the Lord opened the door for Simpson to serve the Chestnut Street Presbyterian Church in Louisville, Kentucky, the Spirit was opening another door. This door was inside the hidden recesses of Simpson's soul. The plight of people needing the Lord took up residence in Simpson's heart. Missions and evangelism would emerge as defining themes in his life and ministry with Christ.

Evangelistic success in Louisville fueled the missionary vision burning within his soul. As the vision grew brighter, he found a restlessness stirring deep within that could not be satisfied through local evangelistic endeavors. Taking the message of Christ to the ends of the earth required a platform, a base of operation, from which the people of other lands could be reached. Living in the heart of Kentucky precluded the possibility of international contact.

Simpson's vision of sharing the gospel with the unreached people of the world clashed with the expectations of the person closest to his heart—his wife Margaret—setting the stage for the most difficult test Simpson had ever faced. Simpson was restless, but Margaret was quite content in Louisville. She felt safe and secure there; it was where she wanted to raise their children. She must have wondered why her husband could not be content to live and serve in the place where God had brought them. Why was his heart consumed with a burning passion that would be disruptive to their home and family? Questions and thoughts such as these must have swirled through her mind as she tried to understand the dream that brought so much troubling uncertainty to her heart and so much confidence to her husband.

Simpson was about to face the greatest challenge the discipline of secrecy every posed to his life. Clashing expectations between a husband and a wife filled the Simpson home with tension and unresolved conflict. How do you move ahead to the place the Spirit is leading when the love of your life isn't convinced that it is the Lord's leading at all? Perhaps the dilemma the Simpsons faced was similar to what Abram and Sarai experienced when the Lord said to Abram, "Leave your country, your people and your father's household and go to the land I will show you" (Genesis 12:1).

God was affirming something to A.B. Simpson's heart and soul that his wife could not sense, let alone see. Why would her husband want to leave the place of God's blessing, a place of growing ministry, to pursue something that may never come to fruition? The answer to that question would not be confirmed to Margaret's heart until long after her husband had accepted the call to serve as the pastor of the Thirteenth Street Presbyterian Church in New York City.

A.B. Simpson embraced the vision from afar. Margaret needed time to gain perspective and understanding of the path God was calling her husband to pursue. Through the transitional process, Simpson sought to uphold his wife in prayer, knowing that as the Lord worked in his heart and life, so the Spirit would work in hers.

Moving ahead in service to Christ and following the vision God implants within the soul does not mean difficulties disappear. In fact, they sometimes intensify. Simpson went to New York to mobilize and lead the Thirteenth Street Presbyterian Church in bringing the good news of Jesus Christ to people living outside the realm of God's saving grace.

It seemed to Simpson that he and the congregation were experiencing a oneness of purpose in this respect. They quickly realized, however, that although they were using the same terms to define the work, their definitions were significantly different. Simpson understood evangelism as taking the message to people needing the Lord. His congregation understood it as sharing the message with people who were like them. Crossing an ethnic, social or cultural boundary was the furthest thing from their minds. They were not anxious to share Christ with people who were different from them.

Simpson viewed the cultural and social diversity surrounding the church as harvest fields of opportunity. In a diary entry from this time he wrote,

> Led to survey my field today, extending especially from 14th St. to 11th, and 6th Avenue to the West side, and my soul filled with joy to find it so great of plain people—whom I love. . . . It is all our own, this field, and God is with us and will bless us. O to please Him fully. . . . Led to think of a letter to all the neighborhood, inviting to the church, but He will show.[6]

His congregation saw a recurrence of the social and cultural pestilence that had threatened the existence of their church a little over a generation before. Uncomfortable with the changing character of their neighborhood, they sought to escape the encroachment surrounding their building on Huston Street, so they relocated to Thirteenth Street. This placed distance—plenty of distance—between the people moving into the neighborhood and the church.[7]

Relocating to Thirteenth Street placed the church in an affluent area of the city, giving the congregation a newfound social and economic prestige. The memories of the way things used to be on Huston Street before "they" started moving in haunted their memories. The congregation had come too far and paid too much to turn their church into a haven for immigrants.

Would their new pastor confine his efforts to the people and things they believed were important, or would he continue trying to reach "them"? Whose approval would Simpson seek? The answer was not long in coming. The presence of over a hundred new believers at a Sunday worship service triggered the conflict. Agitated voices murmured and complained. Who are these people? Where did they come from? Why are they sitting in my pew? Don't they know how to dress or act in a worship service?

These were people Simpson had won to the Lord, who had responded to his service and kindness. This may have made them members of the Lord's Body, but their application to become members of Simpson's congregation was denied. He was forced to find another church for the new converts, one that would welcome and nurture the new Christians his own congregation had turned away.[8]

The congregation's lack of enthusiasm put a damper on Simpson's evangelistic efforts. They wanted him to continue serving as their pastor; they were pleased with the good things God had brought their way. If only their pastor would focus and concentrate his efforts in fulfilling the responsibilities they felt he should pursue! Would Simpson concede to their expectations, or would the vision for world missions and evangelism burning within his heart define the course and direction of his ministry?

Simpson knew the answer to the question. Once again it was the same response given by the Apostle Paul: "If I were still trying to please men, I would not be a servant of Christ" (Galatians 1:10). The vision of reaching people with the message of Christ coupled with his emerging commitment to believers' baptism culminated in Simpson's decision to resign. At Simpson's request, the New York Presbytery dissolved his pastoral relationship with the Thirteenth Street Presbyterian Church and his membership in the Presbytery on November 7, 1881.

Some may wonder why Simpson did not maintain his membership within the Presbytery and pursue evangelistic and missionary outreach under the auspices of the New York Presbytery. Two factors precluded this possibility. In 1880 the New York Presbytery affirmed the need for evangelism among the poor, but did not allocate any funds or personnel to carry out an evangelistic ministry among the unreached masses within the city.[9] The decision not to fund evangelistic ministry to the masses was followed up with a Synod report simply called the *Report on Evange-*

listic Work, which called for a strict reassertion of church control of evangelism.[10]

Even if Simpson had wanted to launch his evangelistic and missionary outreach under the auspices of the Presbytery, he was a pastor without a church who had a vision for ministry that the New York Presbytery did not possess. As the distance between Simpson and the Master's vision for his life became narrower, the distance between Simpson and the denomination he grew up in and served was growing wider. His growing belief in and commitment to believer's baptism sealed the obvious. The Lord was leading Simpson in a direction that involved walking a different path.

FREEDOM FROM THE OPINIONS OF OTHERS

Those who practice the discipline of secrecy have the freedom to live for the Lord's approval. Their steps are not ordered by the impression factor or conditioned by the approval of others. They live with a freedom to say "yes" to Christ even when they do not know where the path is leading, how they will get there or what they will encounter along the way. These are things the Lord will make known to them one step at a time.

Simpson's colleagues questioned the wisdom of his decision to live for the Lord's approval in such an unorthodox manner. To many, evangelizing the multitudes of New York City "looked . . . like a piece of rare folly. . . . It looked like lunacy, and of course there was no lack of comforters to assure him that it was indeed lunacy."[11] Kenneth Mackenzie, an Episcopalian minister and contemporary of Simpson made a similar observation:

> To espouse a cause that had been treated with hostility in all the evangelical communions, was to his friends and critics the guarantee of defeat. . . . He gladly drank the bitter cup, persuaded that he was in the will of God. And it was this impregnable position that won him final favor. Nothing could move him, once he knew the mind of his Lord; nothing could wound him, once he tasted the Lord's goodness.[12]

Every transition in A.B. Simpson's life and ministry was marked by a testing of his ongoing commitment to the discipline of secrecy. He knew that living for the Lord's approval and the Lord's praise is not a one-time event but an ongoing process.

The impression factor and approval addiction meant nothing to Simpson. With the Spirit bearing witness to his spirit, the only things that mattered to Simpson were walking in the will of the Father and having the companionship of Christ.

Is this what matters to you?

CONSIDERATIONS FOR YOUR SPIRITUAL DEVELOPMENT

The acceptance and approval of others plays a formative role in the lives of many people. Approval addiction and the impression factor become a tyrannical, two-headed monster ruling over every thought, decision and action a person makes. Instead of experiencing the joy of living according to the way God has made us, life is scripted by the expectations others have for us.

Practicing the discipline of secrecy frees us to live for God's pleasure. It enables us to pursue the activities that encourage and enable us to develop the abilities and talents we received from God. Secrecy liberates us from the cadence of others' expectations and empowers us to walk in the natural rhythms of God's loving grace.

● ● ● ● ● ● ● ● ● ● ● *Application*

1. Psalm 139:14 says we are "fearfully and wonderfully made." God formed, fashioned and created you. The Lord has given you magnificent talents and abilities. You have the potential to become all that God intends for you to be. By God's design there is only one of you, not two. Pause and thank the Lord for the wonderful creation called you.

2. Your worth and value are not determined by how well you live up to other people's expectations. They are determined by the Creator, and you are absolutely precious in the Lord's eyes. De-

velop a list of the talents and abilities, special interests and gifts God has given to you. Recognize that God has given these to you so you may experience the satisfaction of knowing that He designed you to accomplish something for Christ that no one else can do.

3. Prayerfully develop priorities for living that are consistent with the way God has made you and the way Christ is seeking to lead you.

4. Step-by-step, day-by-day, begin living for the Lord's joy and pleasure. Understand that your resolve to live for the Lord's pleasure will be tested in a variety of ways.

5. It is hard for people to see Jesus when the people who are pointing the way stand in the spotlight, calling attention to themselves. Stand behind the camera and do everything within your power to shine the light on Jesus.

Chapter EIGHT

IT'S ALL ABOUT GOD
The Ultimate Discipline: *Worship*

*W*orship reveals the true nature and disposition of one's heart toward God. In worship we discover what is really taking place in the inner lives of our souls and spirits. It is in worship that we begin to understand our lives in Christ.

Tragically, some think the value of worship is directly related to how it makes them feel. If the experience makes them feel good about themselves or warm and fuzzy inside, then it must be good. They evaluate a worship service by their rating of the message, the performance level of people with leading roles and the latest technology used to capture the senses and stimulate the imagination. And if the size of the crowd is not what they think it should be, nothing else seems to matter.

There are people who would have us believe these things are important. But are they important to God? If so, how valuable are they? Many people are discovering that they are not nearly as important as some imagine them to be.

THE HEART OF WORSHIP

Worship is about the Lord. Worship is the continual response of a heart, a life, touched by the love and grace of God through Jesus Christ. It is the expression of the spirit and soul in responsive harmony and fellowship with God. And worship was the distinguishing quality that characterized the life and ministry of A.B. Simpson. Worship was the spiritual discipline that defined his life and expressed his love and devotion to Jesus Christ, his Lord.

For Simpson, life was all about Jesus, and he expressed this in these words: "Once it was the blessing,/ Now it is the Lord . . ./ All in all forever,/ Jesus will I sing./ Everything in Jesus,/ And Jesus everything."[1] Simpson knew worship, forged in the depths of his life experiences with Christ and welling up from deep within his soul, is all about the Lord.

Developing the spiritual discipline of worship guards the heart, mind, soul and spirit against the dangers of displacing God as sole focus of worship. It keeps worship from becoming a religious experience designed to soothe the emotions, meet our needs or make us feel good about ourselves. These things may happen as a result of a worship experience involving an encounter with Almighty God, but they are not what defines worship. Rather, there is a very real possibility that these things may be closer to the words of Jesus when He quoted the prophet Isaiah, "These people honor me with their lips, but their hearts are far from me. They worship me in vain" (Matthew 15:8-9; cf. Isaiah 29:13), than they are to the heart of worship.

In fact, when Isaiah saw the Lord seated on the throne, a feeling of fear filled his heart and soul. Seeing God's holiness filled every fiber of his being with an acute sense of his sinful unworthiness before the Lord. "Woe to me! . . . I am ruined! For I am a man of unclean lips, and I live among a people of unclean lips, and my eyes have seen the King, the LORD Almighty" (Isaiah 6:5). Isaiah witnessed heavenly worship, the worship of God in His glory. "Holy, holy, holy is the LORD Almighty; the whole earth is full of his glory" (6:3).

Worship involves a sense of expectancy. It anticipates communion with the Father accompanied by the sound of the Lord's voice speaking to our hearts—filling us, changing us, drawing us closer into the presence of Christ.

WORSHIP INVITES SURRENDER

True worship will change us. It is impossible to come into the presence of God—to commune with Him, to hear His voice, to have the Spirit touch our souls—and to remain the same.

Richard Foster makes this observation about worship in *Celebration of Discipline:*

> If worship does not change us, it has not been worship. To stand before the Holy One of eternity is to change. If worship does not propel us to greater obedience, it has not been worship. For just as worship begins in holy expectancy it ends in holy obedience.
>
> Holy obedience saves worship from becoming an . . . escape from the pressing needs of modern life. Worship enables us to hear the call of service clearly so that we respond with the words of Isaiah, "Here I am, send me."
>
> Authentic worship will help us join in the war against the demonic powers everywhere on the personal level, social level, and institutional level. Jesus, Lamb of God, is our Commander and Chief who received His orders for service, "Go in the might and the power of the Lord."[2]

This is what A.B. Simpson did: He went in the might and the power of the Lord to a life of ministry and service for the sake of the gospel of Jesus Christ, taking the message of salvation to the unreached people of the world.

Simpson's life of service and ministry is a reflection of the possibilities that await those who give themselves to God in worship. His was a surrendered life. It was surrendered to God in worship. Day-by-day he embraced the Apostle Paul's admonition to offer his body as a living sacrifice, "holy and pleasing to God—this is your spiritual act of worship" (Romans 12:1). Simpson understood that the heart of worship is more than songs of praise, rejoicing and thanksgiving. The heart of worship is the surrender and the offering up of your heart and life to God. This is when true worship begins.

The Spirit uses everything that precedes this point of surrender and offering—all the various forms of praise and expressions of thanksgiving and gratitude unto the Lord involved with the experience commonly known as worship—to prepare and bring us to the place of surrender. It is at the place called "surrender" that we begin to worship with all of our hearts. It is in surrendering our hearts and lives to the Lord that we enter into the presence of Christ and offer to our Savior a depth of worship that is unknown to those who hold on to their hearts.

Simpson's writings abound with words of encouragement and invitations to follow him into the joyous pleasure and satisfaction of the surrendered life. In *The Fourfold Gospel,* Simpson wrote, "We must make an entire surrender to Him in everything. We must give ourselves to Him thoroughly, definitely, and unconditionally."[3] A continuation of this theme is found in his work *Wholly Sanctified*: "We offer ourselves to God for His absolute ownership, that He may possess us as His peculiar property, prepare us for His purpose and work out in us all His holy and perfect will."[4]

When we surrender ourselves to God in worship, we position ourselves to be used of God in accomplishing His eternal purpose; those who offer words but not their hearts can never come to that place. The life that is yielded to the Lord is open to receive the Spirit's direction and leading. This is the life that will know Christ's way. Simpson affirmed this in *Walking in the Spirit:*

> [The Holy Spirit brings] with Him the manifested presence of the Father and the Son, leading into all truth, guiding in all the will of God, supplying all the needed grace, unfolding the life of Jesus Christ in the believer's daily life, and developing all the fruits of the Spirit in their full variety and complete maturity.[5]

The surrendered heart's concern is Christ. The fulfillment of God's eternal redemptive purpose can now be worked out in and through the surrendered life in a way that is not possible to those who have not given this worship offering to the Lord.

Consequently, it is not surprising to find a new dimension of spiritual conflict emerging as the Enemy seeks to thwart Christ's purpose, prevent the fulfillment of God's will and, if possible, reestablish a footing in the surrendered heart. Simpson understood the reality of this spiritual conflict and cautioned us to guard against it in *Standing on Faith*: "After you consecrate yourself to God, then will come the tug of war . . . the devil will want you to take your will back."[6] Continually surrendering to Christ, living in obedience to the will and the Word and keeping in step with the Spirit are vital elements in withstanding Satan's efforts to keep us from going further and deeper with the Lord.

Satan's efforts may be disguised in the form of a subtle insinuation designed to engender apprehension or reluctance that could cause a willing heart to pause and reconsider a decision formed in faithful obedience to the Word of God or the Spirit's prompting. The slightest hesitation may be the encouragement the Evil One needs to continue pressing, probing, seeking for an advantage.

Nor can we rule out the possibility of a frontal onslaught that threatens to shatter our faith and confidence in Christ with a single blow. Satan launched a series of such assaults against Job in quick succession. Multiple waves of devastating news seared Job's soul with an overwhelming sense of grief. Staggering under the magnitude of his loss, Job found his wife's confidence in the Lord wavering. Even though his soul was filled with anguish over the tragic deaths of his children, Job did not succumb to the Enemy's snare. Instead, Job lifted his face toward heaven and with tear-stained cheeks offered the Lord a sacrifice of praise: "The LORD gave and the LORD has taken away; may the name of the LORD be praised" (Job 1:21). Job responded to the next wave of Satan's assault that left his body racked with excruciating pain by asking, "Shall we accept good from God, and not trouble?" (2:10).

Certainly there were things Job did not understand and could not comprehend. But this one thing he knew: The circumstances of this life would not at that time, nor in the future, cause him to stop offering his life to God. He would continue to offer himself as a "living [sacrifice], holy and pleasing to God" (Romans 12:1).

A.B. Simpson understood the pain that comes to those who consecrate themselves to the Lord. Simpson understood it because he experienced both the subtle insinuations that engendered doubt and the frontal onslaught of Satan's attack. Two incidents from Simpson's life serve to illustrate the dynamics involved in the spiritual tug-of-war he experienced.

The stamina and vitality Simpson needed to vigorously pursue the vision and the calling of God upon his life eluded him. So, throughout the first twenty years of his pastoral ministry, he found it necessary to step away from his ministerial responsibilities for extended periods of time to rest and recuperate.

While at Old Orchard Beach, Maine, Simpson's heart and soul were touched by testimonies of people witnessing to the healing power of Christ in their lives. They affirmed the grace and the sufficiency of God to bring healing to their bodies and to restore the health illness had taken away. As Simpson considered their testimonies and examined the Scriptures, he was convinced that there was another step of surrender he needed to take. That step of surrender involved trusting Christ as his healer, as the One who would meet and care for his physical needs. He described the subtle insinuation that came in his book *The Gospel of Healing:*

> I knew that something was done. Every fiber of my soul was tingling with a sense of God's presence. . . . It was so glorious to believe it simply and to know henceforth, God had it in hand.
>
> Then came the test of faith. The first struck me before I had left the spot. A subtle voice whispered, *Now that you have decided to take God as your Healer, it would help if you should just go down to Dr. Cullis' cottage and get him to pray with you.* I listened to the suggestion for a moment without really thinking. Suddenly, a blow seemed to strike my brain that made me reel as a man stunned.
>
> "Lord, what have I done?" I cried. . . . In a moment the thought came, *That would have been all right before this, but you have just settled this matter forever and told God you will never doubt that it is done.* Immediately I understood what faith meant. . . . I saw that when a thing was settled with God, it was never to be unsettled. When it was done, it was never to be undone or done over again in any sense that could involve a doubt of the finality of the commitment already made. . . .
>
> What the enemy desired was to get some element of doubt about the certainty and completeness of the transaction just closed.[7]

OFFERING OURSELVES

The frontal onslaught in Simpson's spiritual tug-of-war came some time following the death of his four-year-old son, Melville. The lives and future of their children were precious to the Simpsons. Margaret made their well-being her greatest concern. She was not willing to place them in any position that might jeopardize them. The prospects of relocating to New York City from the safe, secure and familiar surroundings in Louisville, Kentucky, was something she was not willing to consider.

The domestic tension and conflict that developed in the Simpson household following Simpson's decision to accept the call to serve the Thirteenth Street Presbyterian Church in New York City is well-documented in the entries he made in his diary. He viewed yielding to his wife's concerns as paramount to scuttling his vision for a global missionary movement. In spiritual terms he could only consider this as disobedience to the Lord's leading. Obviously, Margaret viewed it quite differently. Over time, the conflict was ultimately resolved as the Spirit worked within both of their hearts and lives, answering their prayers for one another.

Presenting ourselves to the Lord as a "living [sacrifice,] holy and pleasing to God" as a "spiritual act of worship" (Romans 12:1) is not a one-time offering. It involves an unending offering of ourselves to God. Moment-by-moment we are faced with the opportunity to make decisions that affirm our commitment and devotion to the Lord. Satan does not want these repeated, and so a spiritual conflict evolves that will test our determination and resolve to live for Jesus.

When Jesus said, "God is spirit, and his worshipers must worship in spirit and in truth" (John 4:24), He was telling us that worship is much more than offering songs of praise, thanksgiving and devotion to the Lord. Certainly these are vital elements in a worship experience that can touch the very fabric of the soul and draw us close to the presence of God. They can prepare our hearts to receive the Lord's message, mercy, grace and forgiveness. But without diminishing the significance of these things in a Christian's life, we have to remember that the heart of worship is about Jesus and about giving our lives to Him as "living sacrifices, holy and pleasing to God."

Those who resolve to live a life of worship for Jesus as living sacrifices enter into a worship experience with God that carries with it transforming power. Tan and Gregg, in *Disciplines of the Holy Spirit,* identify five things the Holy Spirit accomplishes in worship, beginning by directing our focus onto God and away from ourselves.[8]

The evidence in Simpson's life of this resolution is reflected in the titles and the lyrics of hymns and worship songs he composed. The chorus of "Himself" reveals that the focus of Simpson's life was on the Lord: "All in all forever,/ Jesus will I sing./ Everything in Jesus,/ And Jesus everything."[9] Add to this the chorus of "Christ in Me" or the lyrics to "Jesus Only" and we see a declaration of the core beliefs of Simpson's faith in Jesus Christ: "Jesus only, Jesus ever,/ Jesus all in all we sing,/ Savior, Sanctifier, and Healer,/ Glorious Lord and coming King."[10]

Eugene Rivard's "Rediscovering the Music of A.B. Simpson" in Hartzfeld and Nienkirchen's *Birth of a Vision* reveals the role songs of worship and praise played in communicating the core beliefs to people associated with the ministry of Simpson's missionary movement. "[I]t was through singing that the Alliance affirmed, memorized and endeared [the truths contained in "Himself" and "Jesus Only"] to their hearts."[11]

Not only was Simpson's focus centered on God, but he wrote praise-and-worship songs to communicate the importance of a Christ-centered life to people within his missionary movement at home and abroad. Simpson exalted Jesus Christ as Lord of his life, and his songs became a means to encourage others to make Jesus Christ the center of their lives as well.

Simpson's corporate worship experiences were a reflection of what took place in his personal worship in his quiet and private place. Simpson's daughter, in "My Father," shares these insights about her dad's personal devotional life:

> I recall . . . times in the late night watches when I heard him talking to his Lord and wrestling even as Jacob for some blessing, for the lifting of some burden, for the taking of higher ground, for God's help in the sermons of the morrow. At times he would stop praying and burst into song.[12]

Perhaps no greater compliment can be paid to a spiritual leader and servant of Jesus Christ than affirmation from his child that his commitment and devotion in private is the same as it is in public. Added to this are the observations made about A.B. Simpson's corporate worship experience by Mary Agnew Stephens. In her article "Dr. Simpson's Ministry in Song," she wrote,

> Those who knew him intimately were familiar with the glow and thrill of his spirit as he sang over some new hymn which had come to him in a quiet moment alone with God, or during the night watches. . . . Often just before a great service there would be brought forth a hymn throbbing with the message of the great sermon which would follow. How he prized the assistance of any spirit-filled voice that could send forth the message in song.[13]

CONTINUALLY REFRESHING

In public places and behind the scenes, the focus of A.B. Simpson's life was firmly fixed on Jesus Christ.

A second aspect of the transforming power of worship Tan and Gregg identify is the Holy Spirit's working to give us fresh experiences of God's love and mercy.[14] It is not surprising to find that this is a distinguishing characteristic of Simpson's life with Christ. The entries in his diary express his consciousness of God's love and mercy. On the eve of his thirty-sixth birthday, Simpson wrote these words in his diary: "Oh how much He has given me this year. My chief desire, I trust, is the revelation of Jesus as my end, aim, joy, strength and glory."[15] Ten days later he wrote, "Much refreshed with the promise of Christ to be a husband to my heart. Strangely and sweetly conscious of His real imparting to my soul of His love and life as a Husband, that I may bring forth fruit unto Him in souls."[16]

Simpson did not want to live on the memories of what Christ did in his life in the past. He was always anticipating new and fresh encounters with God's love and mercy. One example of this is found in the lyrics of Simpson's song "O Love Divine":

> O Love that gave itself for me,
> Help me to love and live like Thee,
> And kindle in this heart of mine
> The passion fire of love divine.

> O Love divine, O love divine,
> Revive this longing heart of mine,
> And kindle in me from above
> The living fire of heaven's love.[17]

Simpson longed to experience the Lord's love and mercy anew. In *But God* he wrote,

> His chosen sanctuary is the humble and contrite heart where He loves to come to "revive the spirit of the humble and revive the heart of the contrite ones." God is always waiting to meet the devout spirit in the inner chamber of the soul.[18]

Fresh experiences with God's love and mercy are vital reminders of the compelling need to share the message of Christ's salvation with others. Tan and Gregg note that a third dimension of the Holy Spirit's ministry in worship is giving us direction for the future. Since our spirits are more finely tuned to Him when we are in worship, God can speak to us more clearly at that time.[19] God's direction for the future is something spiritual leaders must know. In *Spiritual Leadership*, Henry and Richard Blackaby maintain that

> . . . God is on a mission to redeem humanity. He is the only one who knows how to do it. Leaders must understand, as Christ did, that their role is to seek the Father's will and adjust their lives to Him. . . . Only God can reveal his plans and he does so in his way, on his time schedule, and to whom he wills.[20]

Simpson continually adjusted his life to God's plan. The ministry he pursued flowed from the vision burning in his soul. When Jesus said, "Let us go somewhere else—to the nearby villages—so I can preach there also. That is why I have come" (Mark 1:38), Simpson interpreted it to mean sharing the message with people who have not had the opportunity to hear it. Simpson also understood the implications involved in making the hope of salvation a reality to those without Christ. It meant adjusting his life to the vision so the Father's mission could be fulfilled. Simpson accepted the fact that walking in step with the Spirit's leading involved leaving the boundaries of comfortable surroundings and familiar ways to embrace the new opportunity Christ set before him.

Adjusting his life to God's plan also involved adjusting the methods he used in ministry. He waited upon the Lord to reveal the most effective ways to fulfill His great redemptive purpose in Jesus Christ. If it meant changing how, when and/or where he served, Simpson changed it. He employed innovative strategies and methods that operated "outside the box" in order to reach people beyond the scope of traditional ministries with the message of salvation.

The sound of critics' voices never dissuaded Simpson from adjusting his life to fulfill God's calling. His commitment to reaching the people living beyond the sound of the gospel is expressed in his hymn "My Trust":

> Lord, You have given me a trust,
> A high and holy dispensation;
> To tell the world, and tell I must
> The story of Your great salvation. . . .
>
> Let me be faithful to my trust,
> Telling the world the story. . . .
> Let me be faithful to my trust,
> And use me for Your glory.[21]

When circumstances precluded the possibility of Simpson's going overseas as a missionary, he sought the Lord for other ways to promote and support the cause. His missionary magazines, the founding of a missionary society, the development of a missionary training institute, missionary conferences and conventions are some of the ways Simpson labored to take Christ's message to the unreached people of the world.

The spiritual leader who adjusts his life to God's plan has an additional responsibility. Henry and Richard Blackaby define this responsibility:

> It is to bear witness to what God says. Spiritual leaders must bring followers into a face-to-face encounter with God so they hear from God directly . . . once their people hear from God themselves, there will be no stopping them from participating in the work God is doing.[22]

One of the ways Simpson communicated the vision was through song. He composed numerous missionary and evangelistic songs to express the burden and to share the vision for the ministry Christ gave to him. Titles for these compositions include "Go and Tell," "A Missionary Cry," "Come to Jesus Now," "What Will You Do with Jesus" and "The Regions Beyond." Each of these songs conveys the passion of God's heart for people without Christ and the responsibility of God's people to share the message with them.

Interdenominational missionary conferences and conventions were another way Simpson communicated the vision for reaching people. The Spirit used these missionary conventions to speak directly to the hearts of the people. Their partnership in the gospel was seen in the great numbers who stepped forward to serve at home and abroad and in the promises of financial support for carrying on the work.

CLARITY OF HEART

A fourth dimension of the Spirit's transforming power through worship is the Spirit's revealing the presence of the Enemy and exposing his schemes and devices.[23] Those who live in the presence of Christ and walk in fellowship with the Spirit are able to discern the presence of the Enemy's influence that others may miss. External dangers may be evident to all, but it is the internal danger that poses the greatest threat to one's spiritual vitality and life with Christ. Simpson knew the indispensable value of self-examination, but he also knew that it may not be sufficient to reveal the presence of evil lurking in the secret places. This is why he called upon the Lord to search his heart. This desire is expressed in the lyrics of "Search Me, O God":

> Search me, O God, search me and know my heart.
> Try me and prove me in the hidden part,
> Cleanse me and make me holy as Thou art,
> And lead me in the way everlasting.
>
> Lead me, lead me, lead me in the way everlasting;
> Keep me from the things that wither and decay;
> Give to me the things that cannot pass away—
> And lead me in the way everlasting.[24]

The desire of Simpson's heart was to be clean, pure and holy in the sight of Christ his Savior. He understood that divine empowering and effectiveness for kingdom service was directly related to the purity of his heart before God. By inviting the Lord to search his heart, Simpson guarded his soul and spirit against the possibility of self-deception, rationalization and a host of other things that, if left unchallenged, could mar the beauty of Christ residing within and impair the effectiveness of Simpson's service for the Lord.

Inviting the Lord to search the heart sets the stage to deal with the issues the Lord wants removed or resolved. This naturally leads to confession. Confession is an indispensable preparatory element for those seeking to enter into the heart of worship. In *Whatever Happened to Worship?* A.W. Tozer made this observation:

> No worship is wholly pleasing to God until there is nothing in me displeasing to God. . . . [Y]ou must prepare to worship God, and that preparation is not always pleasant. There may be revolutionary changes which must take place in your life.
>
> If there is to be true and blessed worship, some things in your life must be destroyed, eliminated.[25]

A.B. Simpson did not want to be numbered with those who worship with their lips while their hearts are far from the Lord. He was committed to worshiping the Lord with all of his heart throughout all of his life. "Lord, Reign in Me," "Purify My Heart" and "I Want to Know You" are a sampling of contemporary songs of praise and adoration that express Simpson's passion to live in the presence of Christ.

Simpson never became embroiled in the controversy surrounding worship styles or musical innovations. Darrell Reid, in *Jesus Only*, notes that Simpson believed cultural prejudices were an impediment to true worship and that individual congregations should have the freedom to worship God in the way that is most meaningful to them.[26]

To Simpson, worship was not about styles or preferences; worship was about God. Worship was about the heart living in a right relationship with God and giving to God the adoration, praise, honor and glory that is worthy of the name of the Lord.

As Tan and Gregg note, the final and perhaps culminating evidence of the transforming power of worship are hearts that respond to the Holy Spirit by living in obedience to the Lord.[27] The way we live, our ethics and morals, our concern for others, the attitudes we display, the things we pursue and the priorities we establish stand as the clear and convincing evidences of the reality of our worship and our heart's devotion to Jesus Christ.

In the song "Christ in Me," Simpson expressed it in these words: "Christ in me, Christ in me, Christ in me—O wonderful story! Christ in me, Christ in me, Christ in me, the hope of glory!"[28]

This was what worship was all about to Simpson: It was about the presence of Christ dynamically living within him, and about living in such a way that he shared the deepest intimacy with Christ and so that others could always see that "Christ in me" is the hope of glory.

CONSIDERATIONS FOR YOUR SPIRITUAL DEVELOPMENT

There is a subtle tendency to equate the value of worship with the impression a worship service has or makes upon people. The bigger the impression, the greater the value people attribute to the worship experience. The more people get out of it, the better it is.

Unfortunately, this obscures the central element of worship: Worship is about the Lord. Wholehearted worship is focused on God. It is the expression of the spirit and soul in responsive harmony and fellowship with God. Worship is what we offer to the Lord. The ultimate expression of worship involves giving ourselves as "living sacrifices, holy and pleasing to God."

Worship is not something that is reserved for Sunday. Worship should be a vital element in our daily lives and walks with Christ.

● ● ● ● ● ● ● ● ● ● ● *Application*

Personal Worship

1. Describe the things that are involved in your personal times of worship throughout the week. Which of the elements involved in your personal worship are solely for the Lord's pleasure?

2. When Isaiah saw the Lord, he immediately became aware of the sin in his own life. Has the recognition of God's holiness and glory made you conscious of sin's presence in your life? If so, how did you respond?

3. How has your life changed through a personal encounter with God in worship? What was involved in adjusting your life to God's plan?

Corporate Worship

1. Discuss or think about how the decisions people make Saturday evening affect their readiness to worship God Sunday morning.

2. Describe what is involved in your personal preparation to worship God in a corporate worship service.

3. Do you see yourself as a participant in worship or as an observer? If you see yourself as a participant, describe the level and the depth of your participation.

4. Share how you've sensed God touching your life with a fresh or new sense of His love and grace in worship.

5. Worship involves giving adoration, praise, thanksgiving and gifts to God as expressions of our love and devotion. The one gift God longs for us to give is ourselves. Have you given yourself to the Lord, or is there something holding you back from giving the one gift God longs to receive from you?

A FINAL COMMENT

This examination does not exhaust the formative and ongoing role the spiritual disciplines of engagement and abstinence, in their various forms, played in the formation and development of A.B. Simpson's spiritual life, maturity and ministry. Within his life and ministry we see the Spirit actively working through the spiritual disciplines to mold, shape and form his spiritual character into the likeness of Jesus Christ.

These characteristics were so much a part of his daily walk and relationship with God that there was no reason to call special attention to them. They were qualities the Church of Jesus Christ was well acquainted with, as spiritual disciplines were embraced by men and women who desired more than a mere acquaintance with Christ. In cooperation with the Holy Spirit's working, the spiritual disciplines facilitated the Father's purpose within Simpson's heart and life.

With each step forward, Simpson found that there were things in his life he had to set aside for the sake of the gospel of Jesus Christ. He also discovered areas of his life that had to give way to the uncompromising Lordship of Christ. Spiritual development continued throughout Simpson's days because he learned the secret of the Potter and the clay. The disciplines of the spirit were a means for cooperating with the Lord in fulfilling the purpose God desired. In the process Simpson discovered the one thing he really desired was the Lord.

As we move forward in this new millennium with a vision for the unreached people of the world and a burning passion within our souls to complete Christ's Great Commission, let us embrace the path of spirituality that characterized the life and ministry of A.B. Simpson and those who have gone before.

A Solemn Covenant: The Dedication of Myself to God

Everlasting and almighty God, Ruler of the universe, You made this world and You made me. You are in every place beholding the evil and the good. You see me and know all my thoughts. My innermost thoughts are all familiar to You. You know my motives for coming to You. I appeal to You, Searcher of hearts. So far as I know my heart, it is not a worldly motive that brings me before You now. But my "heart is deceitful above all things, and desperately wicked" [(Jeremiah 17:9, KJV)] and I would not pretend to trust it. You know I have a desire to dedicate myself to You forever. I come before You as a sinner, lost and ruined by the fall, and by my transgressions. Yes, I am the worst of all Your creatures. When I look back on my life, I am filled with shame and confusion. I am ignorant and rude, like an animal in Your sight. Lord, You made Adam holy and happy, and gave him the ability to maintain this state. The penalty of disobedience was death. He disobeyed Your holy law and incurred the penalty. I am his descendent. I have inherited this depravity and this penalty. Your sentence is just. Lord, I bow in submission before You.

Lord, I am an evil person. How can You stoop to look on me? It is an endless deference to even notice me. But truly, Your loving-kindness is boundless and eternal. Lord, You sent Your Son in our image, with a body such as mine and a wise soul. All the perfections of the Godhead abide in Him. So does the modesty of our sinful nature. He is the Mediator of the New Covenant, and through Him we all have access to You by the same Spirit. Through Jesus, the only Mediator, I come to You. Lord, by trusting in His mediation, I boldly approach Your throne of grace. Lord, I feel my own insignificance. But You strengthen me by Your Spirit. I am approaching You to covenant with You for eternal life. In Your Word You told us that it is Your will for all who believe in Your Son to have eternal life. And

You will raise him up on the last day. You gave us a New Covenant and sealed it in Jesus' blood on the cross.

I now declare before You and before my conscience and everything You have created that I accept the conditions of this covenant and close with its terms. I believe on Jesus and accept salvation through Him, my Prophet, Priest and King, as made to me by God, wisdom and righteousness and sanctification. Lord, You made me willing to come to You. By Your love You subdued my rebellious heart. So now take it and use it for Your glory. Whenever rebellious thoughts develop in my heart, overcome them and bring everything that opposes You into subjection to Your authority. I yield myself to You as one alive from the dead, forever. Take and use me for Your glory.

Ratify now in heaven, O my Father, this covenant. Remember it, O Lord, when You bring me to the Jordan. Lord, remember me when You come with all the angels and saints to judge the world. May I be at Your right hand and in heaven with You forever. In heaven write down that I have become Yours, Yours only, and Yours forever. Lord, remember me in the hour of temptation. Never let me depart from this covenant. Lord, I sense my own weakness and so I am not making this in my own strength. If I did, I would fail. But in Your strength, O Captain of my salvation, I shall be strong and more than a conqueror through Christ who loved me.

Lord, I have made this covenant with You according to Your Word. I did not make it for worldly honors or fame, but for eternal life. I know You are true and will never break Your Word. Give to me all the blessings of the New Covenant, especially the Holy Spirit in great abundance. The Spirit is the pledge of my inheritance until the day of redemption. May a double portion of Your Spirit rest upon me. Then I shall proclaim Your ways and laws to transgressors and to Your people. Sanctify me completely and make me fit for heaven. Give me all the spiritual blessings in Christ Jesus.

Now I am a soldier of the Cross and follower of the Lamb. From now on my motto is "I have one King, even Jesus." Support and strengthen me, O my Captain, and be mine forever. Lord, place me in the circumstances You want. If it is in accordance with Your will I request that You give me neither poverty nor riches;

feed me with the food I need, lest I am poor and steal, or lest I become rich and say, "Who is the Lord?" Let Your will be done. Now, give me Your Spirit and protect my heart all the time. Then I will drink of the rivers of salvation, lie down by still waters and be infinitely happy in the favor of my God.

Saturday, January 19, 1861

A Short Biography of A.B. Simpson

*I*n the late 1800s the spiritual awakening sweeping across America changed the way people viewed missions and evangelism. While D.L. Moody's evangelistic fervor captured the hearts of people throughout the nation, A.B. Simpson emerged as the visionary leader who inaugurated a new chapter in modern world missions and evangelism.

A passion for people who had never heard the good news of Jesus Christ burning within Simpson's soul compelled him to enlarge the circle of his ministry. His love for the Church, the Bride of Christ, prompted this Canadian Presbyterian pastor to push beyond the comfortable boundaries of the way things were done. The phenomenal conversion growth of Knox Presbyterian Church in Hamilton, Ontario, set the stage for Simpson to assume the pastoral leadership of the Chestnut Street Presbyterian Church in Louisville, Kentucky, following the Civil War.

Simpson's visionary leadership was the catalyst to healing the strife and the scars the war inflicted upon Louisville. He took the message of God's love and peace beyond church and into the streets. People crowded into theaters on Sunday nights to hear him bring messages that touched the lives of ordinary people who would never think of going to a church on Sunday morning. As Simpson watched them respond to the love of Christ, the Spirit was working within his soul, enlarging his vision and burden for the unreached people of the world.

Convinced that New York City was the strategic place to influence people at home and abroad with the gospel of Jesus Christ, Simpson accepted the call to assume the pastoral leadership of the Thirteenth Street Presbyterian Church. He viewed the neighborhoods surrounding the church as fields ripe unto harvest and sought to mobilize his new congregation to seize the opportunities for the Lord. Unfortunately, some within his church viewed the people in those neighborhoods as an encroaching menace poised to threaten their way of life and worship.

Simpson's passion for the unreached people of the world was a calling of God upon his life that the Thirteenth Street congregation did not possess. Imposing the vision of his heart upon those who were not willing to embrace it could only result in conflict and strife. Sensing their reluctance to move in the direction God was leading him, Simpson resigned to devote the remainder of his life to sharing the message of Christ with the unreached people at home and abroad.

Soon people of kindred spirit and vision surrounded Simpson. They were willing to join hands with him in crossing cultural, social, economic, educational and ethnic barriers to share the love and message of Jesus Christ with others. The ministries they initiated thrived outside the box of traditional church ministry. Countless numbers of people embraced Jesus Christ. As success of these ministries grew, so did the burden to launch a missionary enterprise sending messengers of the good news to the ends of the earth.

The missionary movement founded by A.B. Simpson developed into the global denomination known as The Christian and Missionary Alliance. The Alliance has over 3 million inclusive members in seventy-six nations seeking to share the good news of Jesus Christ with the unreached people of the world.

PLACES OF SIMPSON'S SERVICE AND MINISTRY

Pastoral Ministry

- Knox Presbyterian Church   Hamilton, Ontario   1865-1873
- Chestnut Street
    Presbyterian Church   Louisville, Kentucky   1874-1879
- Thirteenth Street
    Presbyterian Church   New York City, New York   1879-1881
- Gospel Tabernacle   New York City, New York   1881-1919

Publishing

- Editor of *The Gospel in All Lands* (first illustrated missionary
  magazine published in North America)   1880
- Editor of *The Word, Work, and World* (later became *Alliance Life*)   1882
- Founded Christian Alliance Publishing
  Company (now Christian Publications, Inc.)   1883
- Founded The Alliance Press   1890

Education

Founded the Missionary Training Institute (now Nyack College)   1883

Missionary Society

Founded the Christian Alliance   1889
Founded the Evangelical Missionary Alliance   1890
President of The Christian and Missionary Alliance   1897-1919

APPENDIX C

Spiritual Disciplines and
The Christian and Missionary Alliance

*S*impson's pursuit of the spiritual disciplines is exemplified in the lives of the visionary leaders serving in the Alliance today.

In a pastoral letter written nearly a decade ago to official workers, David Rambo, then president of the Alliance, extolled the benefits of the spiritual disciplines and challenged the workers to make the practice of the disciplines a vital element in their continuing spiritual development.

His successor and friend, Paul Bubna, expressed his commitment to the disciplines in the pursuit of knowing and serving Christ. He wrote a statement entitled "My Covenant with God":

> As a new creature in Christ through the finished work of Christ, and as a part of The Christian and Missionary Alliance, I covenant with God to give myself to the following Disciplines in order to hasten the coming of our Lord Jesus Christ through the completing of the Great Commission.
>
> > I will forego my personal, selfish ambitions and yield fully so that He may fill me and work His good will in me.
> >
> > I will set my heart to be an intercessor for the unreached peoples of the earth wherever they may be found.
> >
> > I will pledge to be a steward of all that God puts in my hands with the Great Commission in view.
> >
> > I will become a full participant in the body life of my local church and its endeavors to reach the community where God has planted us.

> I realize that the above commitments may well call for a significant change in lifestyle and values. As God enables me, I will be willing to change and be a change agent in my sphere of influence.

The life of Peter Nanfelt, current president of the Alliance, exemplifies the same commitment to the disciplines in his relationship with Christ and service as Alliance president. It is done in a way that prompts those serving within the Alliance to pause and reflect on the place and the practice of the spiritual disciplines in their own lives.

ENDNOTES

FOREWORD

1. A.B. Simpson, *Is Life Worth Living?* (South Nyack, NY: Christian Alliance Publishing, 1899), p. 29.

INTRODUCTION

1. Keith Bailey, compiler, *The Best of A.B. Simpson* (Harrisburg, PA: Christian Publications, Inc., 1987), p. 39.

CHAPTER ONE

1. A.B. Simpson, *Is Life Worth Living?, p. 29.*
2. Bailey, p. 8.
3. A.B. Simpson, "Breathing Out and Breathing In" (Colorado Springs, CO: A.B. Simpson Historical Library, n.d.). Unpublished poem.
4. David F. Hartzfeld and Charles Nienkirchen, eds., *Birth of a Vision* (Alberta, Canada: Buena Book Services, a division of Horizon House Publishers, 1986), p. 49.
5. A.B. Simpson, *Christ in the Tabernacle* (Camp Hill, PA: Christian Publications, Inc., 1994), p. 72.
6. R. Kent Hughes, *Disciplines of a Godly Man* (Wheaton, IL: Crossway, 1991), p. 16.
7. Bailey, p. 146.
8. A.B. Simpson, *The Old Faith and the New Gospels* (New York: Christian Alliance Publishing Co., 1911), p. 56.
9. A.B. Simpson, *The Self-Life and the Christ-Life* (Camp Hill, PA: Christian Publications, Inc., 1990), pp. 37-8.
10. A.B. Simpson, *But God* (New York: Alliance Press Co., 1899), p. 103.
11. A.B. Simpson, *Life More Abundantly* (New York: Christian Alliance Publishing Co., 1912), p. 55.
12. A.B. Simpson, *But God*, p. 61.
13. A.B. Simpson, *Wholly Sanctified* (Camp Hill, PA: Christian Publications, Inc., 1998), p. 67.
14. A.B. Simpson, *Life More Abundantly*, p. 48.
15. Hartzfeld and Nienkirchen, p. 165.
16. Ibid., p. 166.
17. A.B. Simpson, *The Christ Life* (Camp Hill, PA: Christian Publications, Inc., 1994), pp. 50-1.
18. A.B. Simpson, *Echoes of the New Creation* (New York: Alliance Press Co., 1903), p. 40.
19. A.B. Simpson, *A Larger Christian Life* (Camp Hill, PA: Christian Publications, Inc., 1996), pp. 143-4.
20. Ibid.
21. Hartzfeld and Nienkirchen, p. 186.

22. A.B. Simpson, *Wholly Sanctified*, p. 6.
23. Hartzfeld and Nienkirchen, p. 186.
24. Richard Foster, *Celebration of Discipline* (San Francisco: Harper & Row, 1978, 1988), p. 6.
25. A.B. Simpson, *Wholly Sanctified*, p. 28.
26. Ibid., pp. 12-3.
27. Bailey, p. 57.
28. Ibid.
29. Hartzfeld and Nienkirchen, p. 87.
30. A.B. Simpson, "Search Me, O God," *Hymns of the Christian Life, Volume II* (Camp Hill, PA: Christian Publications, Inc., 1936), 145.

CHAPTER TWO

1. A.B. Simpson, *The Christ Life*, p. 38.
2. Ibid., p. 73.
3. A.B. Simpson, *My Own Story*, (Colorado Springs, CO: A.B. Simpson Historical Library, n.d.), p. 9. Unpublished personal reflections of A.B. Simpson.
4. Ibid., pp. 9-10.
5. A.B. Simpson, *A Solemn Covenant: The Dedication of Myself to God* (Colorado Springs, CO: A.B. Simpson Historical Library, 1861).
6. A.B. Simpson, *Wholly Sanctified*, p. 13.
7. Ibid., p. 34.
8. A.B. Simpson, *The Holy Spirit: Power from on High* (Camp Hill, PA: Christian Publications, Inc., 2003), p. 317.
9. A.B. Simpson, *Is Life Worth Living?*, p. 29.
10. A.B. Simpson, *The Christ Life*, p. 26.
11. Ibid., p. 42.
12. A.B. Simpson, *Wholly Sanctified*, pp. 14-5.
13. Hartzfeld and Nienkirchen, p. 10.
14. A.B. Simpson, "A Personal Witness," *The Alliance Weekly*, October 2, 1915, quoted in Hartzfeld and Nienkirchen, pp. 111-2.
15. A.B. Simpson, *Wholly Sanctified*, p. 31.
16. Darrel Reid, "Jesus Only: The Early Life and Presbyterian Ministry of Albert Benjamin Simpson, 1843-1911" (Ph.D. diss., Queen's University, Kingston, Ontario, Canada, 1994), p. 247.
17. Ibid., p. 236.
18. Ibid., p. 240.
19. A.E. Thompson, *A.B. Simpson: His Life and Work* (Harrisburg, PA: Christian Publications, Inc., 1920), p. 151.
20. A.B. Simpson, *Wholly Sanctified*, p. 69.
21. A.B. Simpson, *Life More Abundantly*, p. 49.
22. A.B. Simpson, *The Christ Life*, p. 55.
23. A.B. Simpson, *Wholly Sanctified*, pp. 44-5.
24. Ibid., pp. 48-9.
25. Thompson, pp. 22-3.
26. A.B. Simpson, *Standing on Faith* (London: Marshall, Morgan & Scott, 1932), pp. 109-10.

27. *Christ Our Sanctifier* (New York: The Christian and Missionary Alliance, n.d.). A tract highlighting Alliance views on sanctification.

28. Emma Beere, comp., "Simpson Anecdotes," as found in C. Donald McKaig's unpublished *Simpson Scrapbook* (Colorado Springs, CO: A.B. Simpson Historical Library, n.d.), p. 238.

29. Robert L. Niklaus, John S. Sawin and Samuel J. Stoesz, *All for Jesus: God at Work in The Christian and Missionary Alliance over One Hundred Years* (Camp Hill, PA: Christian Publications, Inc., 1986), p. 135.

30. Emma Beere, "Dr. Simpson's Ministry Through Books and Pamphlets," as found in McKaig, p. 314.

31. A.B. Simpson, "In His Heart and Hand," *Songs of the Spirit* (Harrisburg, PA: Christian Publications, Inc., n.d.), pp. 58-9.

CHAPTER THREE

1. Reid, p. 158.

2. Kenneth Mackenzie, "My Memories of Dr. Simpson," *The Alliance Weekly,* September 11, 1937.

3. Harold H. Simpson, *Cavendish: Its History, Its People. The Development of a Community from Wilderness to World Recognition with a Broad Outreach to Major Landmarks in the Prince Edward Island Story* (Charlottetown, PEI: the Author, 1973), p. 187.

4. A.B. Simpson, *My Own Story,* p. 7.

5. Ibid., p. 5.

6. Ibid., p. 6.

7. Ibid., p. 7.

8. A.B. Simpson, *The Life of Prayer* (Camp Hill, PA: Christian Publications, Inc., 1996), p. 34.

9. Mackenzie, "My Memories of Dr. Simpson," September 11, 1937.

10. A.B. Simpson, *The Life of Prayer,* p. 76.

11. A.B. Simpson, *Himself* (Camp Hill, PA: Christian Publications, Inc., 2000), p. 10.

12. A.B. Simpson, *The Life of Prayer,* p. 74.

13. Ibid., p. 64.

14. Ibid.

15. Ibid., p. 80.

16. Ibid., p. 85.

17. Ibid.

18. A.B. Simpson, *The Christ Life,* p. 56.

19. A.B. Simpson, *The Life of Prayer*, p. 15.

20. Ibid., p. 18.

21. A.B. Simpson, *Called to Serve at Home* (Harrisburg, PA: Christian Publications, Inc., n.d.), p. 11.

22. Ibid., p. 14.

23. A.B. Simpson, *The Love-Life of the Lord* (Harrisburg, PA: Christian Alliance Publishing Co., n.d.), p. 51.

24. A.B. Simpson, *Christ in the Tabernacle,* pp. 75-6.

25. A.B. Simpson, *The Life of Prayer,* pp. 17-8.

26. Ibid., p. 51.

27. Ibid., p. 47.

28. Ibid., p. 51.

29. A.B. Simpson, *Christ in the Tabernacle*, p. 22.

30. Robert Ekvall, "A Missionary Statesman," *The Alliance Weekly*, July 10, 1937.

31. A.B. Simpson, *The Christ Life*, pp. 53-4.

32. A.B. Simpson, *The Life of Prayer*, p. 17.

33. Ibid., p. 40.

34. A.B. Simpson, *Christ in the Tabernacle*, pp. 87-8.

35. A.B. Simpson, *Diary* (Colorado Springs, CO: A.B. Simpson Historical Library),
    December 16, 1879.

36. A.B. Simpson, *Days of Heaven on Earth* (Camp Hill, PA: Christian Publications, Inc.,
    1984), February 16.

37. A.B. Simpson, *The Holy Spirit*, p. 160.

38. Mackenzie, "My Memories of Dr. Simpson," September 11, 1937.

39. A.B. Simpson, "The Secret of Prayer," *Living Truths 4*, March 1904, p. 121.

40. Ibid., pp. 125-6.

41. William MacArthur, "Dr. Simpson's Methods" as found in McKaig,
    p. 322.

42. A.B. Simpson, *The Life of Prayer*, p. 36.

43. Ibid., p. 118.

44. Thompson, p. 50.

45. Reid, p. 267; see also Thompson, p. 54.

46. A.B. Simpson, *Diary*, November 28, 1879.

47. Ibid., November 10, 1879.

48. Ibid., November 14, 1879.

49. Ibid., November 25, 1879.

50. Ibid., November 24, 1879.

51. Ibid., November 25, 1879.

52. Thompson, p. 85.

53. Ibid., p. 88.

54. Ibid., p. 91.

55. Ibid., p. 98.

56. Ibid., pp. 185-6.

57. Ibid., pp. 188-9.

58. Paul Rader, "Foreword: A Eulogy to A.B. Simpson," as found in McKaig, p. 355.

59. "In Memorial," *The Alliance Weekly*, November 1, 1919.

CHAPTER FOUR

1. Eugene H. Peterson, *Under the Unpredictable Plant* (Grand Rapids, MI: Eerdmans,
   1992), p. 109.

2. John Maxwell, *The 21 Irrefutable Laws of Leadership* (Nashville, TN: Nelson
   Publishers, 1998), p. 188.

3. A.B. Simpson, *A Larger Christian Life*, pp. 62-3.

4. A.B. Simpson, *Standing on Faith*, p. 99.

5. A.B. Simpson, *The Christ Life*, p. 62.

6. A.B. Simpson, *The Self-Life and the Christ-Life*, p. 3.

7. A.B. Simpson, "Distinctive Teachings," *The Word, Work, and World*, July 1887, p. 3.

8. A.B. Simpson, *The Self-Life and the Christ-Life*, p. 5.

9. A.B. Simpson, *The Self Life and The Christ Life* (New York: Christian Alliance Publishing Co., n.d.), p. 11. Note: An older edition of this book was used in this instance for clarity of wording.

10. A.B. Simpson, *Standing on Faith*, p. 105.

11. Thompson, p. 151.

12. A.B. Simpson, *The Fourfold Gospel* (Camp Hill, PA: Christian Publications, Inc., 2003), pp. 74-5.

13. Bailey, p. 55.

14. A.B. Simpson, *The Fourfold Gospel*, p. 21.

15. A.B. Simpson, *Walking in the Spirit* (New York: Alliance Press Co., 1890), pp. 53-4.

16. A.B. Simpson, *The Love-Life of the Lord*, p. 55.

17. A.B. Simpson, *The Self-Life and the Christ-Life*, p. 50.

18. A.B. Simpson, *The Gospel of Healing* (Camp Hill, PA: Christian Publications, Inc., 1994), pp. 71-2.

19. A.B. Simpson, *My Own Story*, p. 10.

20. Thompson, p. 41.

21. A.W. Tozer, *Wingspread: A Study in Spiritual Altitude* (Camp Hill, PA: Christian Publications, Inc., 1997), p. 39.

22. Thompson, p. 41.

23. A.B. Simpson, *Diary*, November 14, 1879.

24. Ibid., November 17, 10, 25 and December 1, 1879.

25. Ibid., December 19, 1879.

26. Reid, p. 356. Reid notes that Simpson's starting salary at the Broadway Tabernacle in Louisville, Kentucky, five years earlier, was $5,000. The Thirteenth Street Presbyterian Church offered Simpson a salary of $3,500. The move to New York City involved at least a twenty-five percent reduction in compensation.

27. A.B. Simpson, *Diary*, December 16, 1879.

28. Tozer, *Wingspread*, p. 122.

29. Thompson, p. 167.

30. Tozer, *Wingspread*, p. 124.

31. Ibid.

32. Kenneth Mackenzie, *The After Glow of a Sun-lit Life, A Eulogy of A.B. Simpson* (Colorado Springs, CO: A.B. Simpson Historical Library, 1919), n.p.

33. Tozer, *Wingspread*, p. 97.

34. Ibid., p. 56.

35. Mackenzie, *The After Glow of a Sun-lit Life*, n.p.

36. Ibid.

37. George Sandison, *A Eulogy to A.B. Simpson* (Colorado Springs, CO: A.B. Simpson Historical Library, 1919), n.p.

CHAPTER FIVE

1. Siang-Yang Tan and Douglas H. Gregg, *Disciplines of the Holy Spirit* (Grand Rapids, MI: Zondervan, 1997), p. 179.

2. Foster, p. 75.

3. Reid, p. 123.

4. Thompson, p. 58.

5. A.B. Simpson, "The Gospel Tabernacle," *The Word, Work, and World*, March 1883.

6. *Minutes of the General Council of The Christian and Missionary Alliance* (Nyack, New York, 1914).

7. Ekvall.

8. Kenneth Mackenzie, "My Memories of Dr. Simpson," *The Alliance Weekly,* May 22, 1937.

9. W.R. Moody, *A Eulogy of A.B. Simpson* (Colorado Springs, CO: A.B. Simpson Historical Library, 1919), n.p.

CHAPTER SIX

1. A.W. Tozer, *That Incredible Christian* (Camp Hill, PA: Christian Publications, Inc., 1998), p. 151.

2. A.B. Simpson, *A Solemn Covenant.*

3. Thompson, p. 197.

4. Ibid.

5. Ibid.

6. Reid, p. 437.

7. Tozer, *Wingspread,* pp. 49-50.

8. Reid, p. 427.

9. Ibid., p. 432.

10. A.B. Simpson, *A Solemn Covenant.*

11. A.B. Simpson, *The Holy Spirit,* p. 536.

12. Reid, p. 309.

13. Harry Verploegh, comp. and ed., *A.W. Tozer: An Anthology* (Camp Hill, PA: Christian Publications, Inc., 1984), p. xi.

14. A.B. Simpson, *The Holy Spirit,* p. 159.

15. A.B. Simpson, *The Power of Stillness* as quoted by Beere in "Simpson Anecdotes," as found in McKaig, pp. 233-4.

16. A.B. Simpson, *The Holy Spirit,* p. 160.

17. Ibid., p. 361.

18. Ibid., p. 368.

19. A.B. Simpson, *A Larger Christian Life,* p. 37.

20. Foster, p. 91.

21. A.W. Tozer, *That Incredible Christian,* p. 149.

22. Ibid., pp. 150-1.

23. Ibid., p. 151.

24. Reid, pp. 178-9.

25. A.B. Simpson, letter written aboard the *Peruvian* off the coast of Ireland to Mrs. Margaret Simpson (Colorado Springs, CO: A.B. Simpson Historical Library, n.d.), May 16, 1871.

26. Ibid., Venice, June 18, 1871.

27. Ibid., Geneva, July 2, 1871.

28. Thompson, p. 65.

29. Ibid., pp. 65-6.

30. A.B. Simpson, *The Fullness of Jesus* (New York: Christian Alliance Publishing Co., 1890), p. 66.

31. Thompson, pp. 67-8. Thompson's quote is from Simpson's sermon series entitled *The Christ of the Forty Days.* These messages were preached at the Gospel Tabernacle,

New York City, New York, between Easter and May 18, 1890. The series was later compiled into a book by the same title and published by the Christian Alliance Publishing Company, New York. No publication date is given. Christian Publications, Inc. continues to produce *The Christ of the Forty Days*.

32. A.B. Simpson, "Himself," *Voices in Worship: Hymns of the Christian Life* (Camp Hill, PA: Christian Publications, Inc., 2003), 303.
33. Emma Beere, comp., "Simpson Anecdotes," as found in McKaig, pp. 231-2.
34. Ibid., pp. 232-3.
35. Thompson, pp. 68-9.
36. Beere, "Simpson Anecdotes," as found in McKaig, p. 231.
37. "Dr. Simpson's Sermon," *Louisville [Kentucky] Courier-Journal,* January 14, 1878. Quoted by Reid, p. 335.
38. A.B. Simpson, *The Gospel of Healing,* p. 123.
39. Ibid., p. 124.
40. A.B. Simpson, *Diary,* January 4 and 12 and February 1, 1880.
41. A.B. Simpson, *The Gospel of Healing,* pp. 120-1.
42. Ibid., p. 122.
43. Ibid.
44. Ibid., pp. 124-5.
45. Ibid., p. 126.
46. Ibid., pp. 130-1.
47. Beere, "Simpson Anecdotes," as found in McKaig, p. 231.

CHAPTER SEVEN

1. John Ortberg, *The Life You've Always Wanted* (Grand Rapids, MI: Zondervan, 1997), p. 158.
2. Leighton Ford, *Transforming Leadership* (Downers Grove, IL: InterVarsity Press, 1993), p. 106.
3. Dallas Willard, *Spirituality and Ministry Notebook* (Pasadena, CA: Fuller Theological Seminary, 1994), p. 19.
4. Thompson, p. 41.
5. Reid, p. 166.
6. A.B. Simpson, *Diary,* November 26, 1879.
7. Reid, p. 347.
8. Samuel J. Stoesz, *Understanding My Church* (Harrisburg, PA: Christian Publications, Inc., 1983), p. 105.
9. Reid, p. 369.
10. Ibid., p. 385.
11. Tozer, *Wingspread,* p. 86.
12. Mackenzie, *The After Glow of a Sun-lit Life.*

CHAPTER EIGHT

1. A.B. Simpson, "Himself," *Voices in Worship,* 303.
2. Foster, p. 148.
3. A.B. Simpson, *The Fourfold Gospel,* p. 29.
4. A.B. Simpson, *Wholly Sanctified,* p. 12.

5. A.B. Simpson, *Walking in the Spirit*, p. 26.
6. A.B. Simpson, *Standing on Faith*, p. 102.
7. A.B. Simpson, *The Gospel of Healing*, pp. 126-7.
8. Tan and Gregg, p. 151.
9. A.B. Simpson, "Himself."
10. A.B. Simpson, "Jesus Only," *Voices in Worship*, 300.
11. Hartzfeld and Nienkirchen, p. 85.
12. Margaret Buckman, "My Father," as found in McKaig, p. 262.
13. Mary Agnew Stephens, "Dr. Simpson's Ministry in Song," as found in McKaig, p. 317.
14. Tan and Gregg, p. 152.
15. A.B. Simpson, *Diary*, December 14, 1879.
16. Ibid., December 23, 1879.
17. A.B. Simpson, "O Love Divine," *Voices in Worship*, 460.
18. A.B. Simpson, *But God*, pp. 106-7.
19. Tan and Gregg, p. 152.
20. Henry and Richard Blackaby, *Spiritual Leadership* (Nashville, TN: Broadman and Holman, 2001), p. 70.
21. A.B. Simpson, "My Trust," *Voices in Worship*, 554.
22. Blackaby and Blackaby, p. 75.
23. Tan and Gregg, p. 152.
24. A.B. Simpson, "Search Me, O God," *Hymns of the Christian Life, Volume II* (1936), 145.
25. A.W. Tozer, *Whatever Happened to Worship?* (Camp Hill, PA: Christian Publications, Inc., 1985), p. 125.
26. Reid, p. 191.
27. Tan and Gregg, p. 153.
28. A.B. Simpson, "Christ in Me," *Voices in Worship*, 297.

BIBLIOGRAPHY

Bailey, Keith. comp. *The Best of A.B. Simpson*. Harrisburg, PA: Christian Publications, Inc., 1987.

Beere, Emma. "Dr. Simpson's Ministry Through Books and Pamphlets," as found in C. Donald McKaig's unpublished *Simpson Scrapbook*. Colorado Springs, CO: A.B. Simpson Historical Library, n.d. Photocopy.

———. comp. "Simpson Anecdotes," as found in C. Donald McKaig's unpublished *Simpson Scrapbook*. Colorado Springs, CO: A.B. Simpson Historical Library, n.d. Photocopy.

Benson, Bob Sr. and Michael W. Benson. *Disciplines for the Inner Life*. Nashville, TN: Generoux/Nelson, 1989.

Blackaby, Henry and Richard. *Spiritual Leadership*. Nashville, TN: Broadman and Holman, 2001.

Boardman, William. *The Higher Christian Life*. Harrisburg, PA: Sprinkle Publications, 1996.

Bubna, Paul. *A Heart for God*. Colorado Springs, CO: The Christian and Missionary Alliance, 1998.

Christ Our Sanctifier. New York: The Christian and Missionary Alliance, n.d.

Ekvall, Robert. "A Missionary Statesman," *The Alliance Weekly*, July 10, 1937.

Ford, Leighton. *Transforming Leadership*. Downers Grove, IL: InterVarsity Press, 1993.

Foster, Richard. *Celebration of Discipline*. San Francisco: Harper & Row, 1978, 1988.

Grubbs, Francis. "Nomination Speech for President of The Christian and Missionary Alliance." Presented at the General Council of The Christian and Missionary Alliance. Milwaukee, WI, May 29, 1998.

Hartzfeld, David and Charles Nienkirchen. eds. *Birth of a Vision*. Alberta, Canada: Buena Book Services, a division of Horizon House Publishers, 1986.

Hughes, R. Kent. *Disciplines of a Godly Man*. Wheaton, IL: Crossway, 1991.

"In Memorial," *The Alliance Weekly*, November 1, 1919.

Mackenzie, Kenneth. *The After Glow of a Sun-lit Life, A Eulogy of A.B. Simpson*. Photocopy, original held at A.B. Simpson Historical Library, Colorado Springs, CO, 1919.

———. "My Memories of Dr. Simpson," *The Alliance Weekly,* May 22, 1937.

———. "My Memories of Dr. Simpson," *The Alliance Weekly,* September 11, 1937.

Maxwell, John. *The 21 Irrefutable Laws of Leadership.* Nashville, TN: Nelson Publishers, 1998.

McKaig, C. Donald. *Simpson Scrapbook.* Unpublished. Original held at A.B. Simpson Historical Library, Colorado Springs, CO, n.d.

Minutes of the General Council of The Christian and Missionary Alliance. Nyack, New York, 1914.

Moody, W.R. *A Eulogy of A.B. Simpson.* Photocopy, original held at A.B. Simpson Historical Library, Colorado Springs, CO, 1919.

Nanfelt, Peter. "The Nonnegotiables of an Alliance Movement," *Completing Christ's Great Commission—Reflections from the President to Coworkers in Ministry.* Colorado Springs, CO, August 1999.

Niklaus, Robert L., John S. Sawin and Samuel J. Stoesz. *All for Jesus: God at Work in The Christian and Missionary Alliance over One Hundred Years.* Camp Hill, PA: Christian Publications, Inc., 1986.

Ortberg, John. *The Life You've Always Wanted.* Grand Rapids, MI: Zondervan, 1997.

Peterson, Eugene. *Under the Unpredictable Plant.* Grand Rapids, MI: Eerdmans, 1992.

Rader, Paul. "Foreword: Eulogy of A.B. Simpson,"as found in C. Donald McKaig's unpublished *Simpson Scrapbook.* Colorado Springs, CO: A.B. Simpson Historical Library, n.d. Photocopy.

Reid, Darrel. "Jesus Only: The Early Life and Presbyterian Ministry of Albert Benjamin Simpson, 1843-1911," Ph.D. diss., Queen's University, Kingston, ON, Canada, 1994.

Sandison, George. "A Eulogy to A.B. Simpson." Photocopy, original held at A.B. Simpson Historical Library, Colorado Springs, CO, 1919.

Simpson, A.B. "Breathing Out and Breathing In." Photocopy of an unpublished poem, original held at A.B. Simpson Historical Library, Colorado Springs, CO, n.d.

———. *But God.* New York: Alliance Press Co., 1899.

———. *Called to Serve at Home.* Harrisburg, PA: Christian Publications, Inc., n.d.

———. "Christ in Me," *Voices in Worship: Hymns of the Christian Life.* Camp Hill, PA: Christian Publications, Inc., 2003.

———. *Christ in the Tabernacle.* Camp Hill, PA: Christian Publications, Inc., 1994.

———. *The Christ Life.* Camp Hill, PA: Christian Publications, Inc., 1994.

———. *Days of Heaven on Earth.* Harrisburg, PA: Christian Publications, Inc., 1984.

———. *Diary.* Photocopy, original held at A.B. Simpson Historical Library, Colorado Springs, CO, 1878-1880.

———. "Distinctive Teachings," *The Word, Work, and World,* July 1887.

———. "Dr. Simpson's Sermon," *Louisville* [Kentucky] *Courier-Journal,* January 14, 1878.

———. *Echoes of the New Creation.* New York: Alliance Press Co., 1903.

———. *The Fourfold Gospel.* Camp Hill, PA: Christian Publications, Inc., 2003.

———. *The Fullness of Jesus.* New York: Christian Alliance Publishing Co., 1890.

———. *The Gospel of Healing.* Camp Hill, PA: Christian Publications, Inc., 1994.

———. "The Gospel Tabernacle," *The World, Work, and World,* March 1883.

———. *Himself.* Camp Hill, PA: Christian Publications, Inc., 2000.

———. "Himself," *Voices in Worship: Hymns of the Christian Life.* Camp Hill, PA: Christian Publications, Inc., 2003.

———. *The Holy Spirit: Power from on High.* Camp Hill, PA: Christian Publications, Inc., 2003.

———. "In His Heart and Hand," *Songs of the Spirit.* Harrisburg, PA: Christian Publications, Inc., n.d.

———. *Is Life Worth Living?* South Nyack, NY: Christian Alliance Publishing, 1899.

———. "Jesus Only," *Voices in Worship: Hymns of the Christian Life.* Camp Hill, PA: Christian Publications, Inc., 2003.

———. *A Larger Christian Life.* Camp Hill, PA: Christian Publications, Inc., 1996.

———. Letters to Mrs. Margaret Simpson. Photocopies, originals held at A.B. Simpson Historical Library, Colorado Springs, CO, May 16, 1871, June 18, 1871 and July 2, 1871.

———. *Life More Abundantly.* New York: Christian Alliance Publishing Co., 1912.

———. *The Life of Prayer.* Camp Hill, PA: Christian Publications, Inc., 1996.

———. *The Love-Life of the Lord.* Harrisburg, PA: Christian Alliance Publishing Co., n.d.

———. "My Own Story." Photocopy, original held at A.B. Simpson Historical Library, Colorado Springs, CO, n.d.

———. "My Trust," *Voices in Worship: Hymns of the Christian Life.* Camp Hill, PA: Christian Publications, Inc., 2003.

———. "O Love Divine," *Voices in Worship: Hymns of the Christian Life.* Camp Hill, PA: Christian Publications, Inc., 2003.

———. *The Old Faith and the New Gospels.* New York: Christian Alliance Publishing Co., 1911.

————. "A Personal Witness," *The Alliance Weekly*. October 2, 1915, quoted in David Hartzfeld and Charles Nienkirchen, *Birth of a Vision*. Alberta, Canada: Buena Book Services, a division of Horizon House Publishers, 1986.

————. *The Power of Stillness*. New York: Christian Alliance Publishing Co., n.d.

————. "Search Me, O God," *Hymns of the Christian Life, Volume II.* Camp Hill, PA: Christian Publications, Inc., 1936.

————. "The Secret of Prayer," *Living Truths 4,* March 1904.

————. *The Self-Life and the Christ-Life*. Camp Hill, PA: Christian Publications, Inc., 1990.

————. *The Self Life and The Christ Life*. New York: Christian Alliance Publishing Co., n.d.

————. *A Solemn Covenant: The Dedication of Myself to God*. Photocopy, original held at A.B. Simpson Historical Library, Colorado Springs, CO, 1861.

————. *Standing on Faith*. London: Marshall, Morgan & Scott, 1932.

————. *Walking in the Spirit*. New York: Alliance Press Co., 1890.

————. *Wholly Sanctified*. Camp Hill, PA: Christian Publications, Inc., 1998.

Simpson, Harold H. *Cavendish: Its History, Its People. The Development of a Community from Wilderness to World Recognition with a Broad Outreach to Major Landmarks in the Prince Edward Island Story*. Charlottetown, PEI: the Author, 1973.

Stoesz, Samuel J. *Understanding My Church*. Harrisburg, PA: Christian Publications, Inc., 1983.

Tan, Siang-Yang and Douglas H. Gregg. *Disciplines of the Holy Spirit*. Grand Rapids, MI: Zondervan, 1997.

Thompson, A.E. *A.B. Simpson: His Life and Work*. Harrisburg, PA: Christian Publications, Inc., 1920.

Tozer, A.W. *That Incredible Christian*. Camp Hill, PA: Christian Publications, Inc., 1998.

————. *Whatever Happened to Worship?* Camp Hill, PA: Christian Publications, Inc., 1985.

————. *Wingspread: A Study in Spiritual Altitude*. Camp Hill, PA: Christian Publications, Inc., 1997.

Verploegh, Harry. comp. and ed. *A.W. Tozer: An Anthology*. Camp Hill, PA: Christian Publications, Inc., 1984.

Willard, Dallas. *The Spirit of the Disciplines*. San Francisco: Harper & Row, 1988.

————. *Spirituality and Ministry Notebook*. Pasadena, CA: Fuller Theological Seminary, 1994.